LANGUAGE ARTS

Grade 2

Credits:
McGraw-Hill Children's Publishing Editorial/Production Team
Vincent F. Douglas, B.S. and M. Ed.
Tracey E. Dils
Jennifer Blashkiw Pawley
Teresa A. Domnauer
Amy Mayr

Big Tuna Trading Company Art/Editorial/Production Team
Mercer Mayer
John R. Sansevere
Erica Farber
Brian MacMullen
Matthew Rossetti
Linda Hayward
Kamoon Song
Soojung Yoo

Children's Publishing

Send all inquiries to: McGraw-Hill Children's Publishing, 8787 Orion Place, Columbus OH 43240-4027

1-57768-842-2

2 3 4 5 6 7 8 9 10 QPD 06 05 04 03 02

The McGraw-Hill Companies

WELCOME TO CRITTERVILLE!
Spider
Frog
Grasshopper
Mouse
Little Critter
Little Sister
Dad
Kitty
Mom
Blue
Gator
Bat Child
Gabby
Bun Bun
Tiger
Maurice
Molly
Malcolm

LANGUAGE ARTS

Grade 2

Table of Contents

Grammar Challenge

Become a Writing Detective!

A good writer is also a detective. A good writer examines each sentence. When something isn't exactly right, a good writer decides how to fix it and makes a mark.

When you are working in this workbook and on other work you do, you need to make sure you always go back and look over your work to see if anything should be corrected.

Pretend you are a detective looking for clues. A writing detective is called a proofreader. Proofreaders use special marks to show that something should be fixed. You can use these special editing marks, too.

Three lines ≡ underneath a letter mean that the letter should be capitalized.

i am going to the zoo. → I am going to the zoo.

If you need to add a period, then use this mark ⊙

Little Critter has a dog⊙ → Little Critter has a dog.

Proofreader's Toolbox

lowercase: . . . . /
capitalize: . . . . ≡
add a comma: . . . . ,
add a period: . . . . ⊙
add a quotation mark: . . . "
add an apostrophe: . . . . . '

First Word in a Sentence

Use a capital letter to begin each sentence. The capital is like a sign that says "START HERE."

The capital letter at the beginning of each sentence tells you that it is time to begin a new thought.

Little Critter wrote a story. Help him proofread the first paragraph. Write this mark ≡ to show the letters that should be capitalized. Write the capital letters above.

mouse is a great pet. he likes to run all around my room.

sometimes I let him ride in my pocket. he lives in a cage on

my bookshelf. mouse enjoys running on his exercise wheel.

he likes to shred

up paper to make

a soft bed. mouse

is my friend.

Read Gabby's story about an unhappy bird. Use this mark ≡ to show the four letters that should be capitalized. Write a capital letter above each one.

Example: they are going to the store to buy some milk.

The little bird was lost. first, he flew to a pine tree. then he flew to an oak tree. finally, he heard his mother's chirp. then he knew just where to fly.

Write two sentences about the picture. Begin each sentence with a capital letter.

1. ______________________________

2. ______________________________

The Word I

The word **I** is always a capital letter.

You are a very important person. When you use **I** in place of your name, make it a capital letter.

I love sports!

My friends and I play soccer.

Playing soccer is something I like to do.

Tiger wrote a poem. Use this mark ≡ to show each letter that should be a capital letter. Write the capital letter above each one.

My friend and i went hiking.

We walked down River Road.

i found a caterpillar,

and then i caught a toad.

My friend dug up some worms.

i helped him dig the hole.

We could be catching lots of fish,

if i just had a pole.

Read Little Critter's riddles below. Use this mark ≡ to show the six letters that should be capitalized. Write the capital letter above each one.

- I am an insect and i can do what I am. What am i ?

  i am a fly!

- i am round on the ends and high in the middle. What am i ?

  i am Ohio!

Pretend you are a football or soccer player. Write two sentences about what you would be doing. Use capital letters where they are needed.

1. ______________________________

2. ______________________________

Handwriting Check

Look at your handwriting above. Are your words sitting on the line? Did you take your time and use your best handwriting? Did you put spaces between your words? Do your tall letters touch the top line and your small letters fit between the dotted and the lower lines?

How did you do? (circle one)

Great!

Good!

O.K.

I'll do better next time.

People and Pets

A person's (or a critter's) name, or a pet's name always begins with a capital letter.

Little Critter took his dog Blue for a walk in the park. He saw Molly and Maurice on the swings.

Draw a picture of someone you know with his or her pet. Write your friend's name and the animal's name under the picture.

Write a sentence about your picture. Use names in your sentence.

Little Critter has lots of pets. Pretend you are Little Critter, and give all of your pets different names. Begin each name with a capital letter.

Write the names of six people you know. Use a capital letter for the first letter of every name.

1. Mom
2. Dad
3. Corinne.P.
4. Isabel.P.
5. Amelia.P.
6. Sarah.W.

Titles of Respect

Miss, Mrs., Ms., and Mr. are titles of respect and should be used before certain names. Begin each title with a capital letter.

Use the proofreader's mark to show the letters that should be capitalized. Write the capital letter above.

Miss Kitty

ms. Dingo   mr. Hogley   mrs. Critter

Draw a picture of an adult you know. Write that person's name on the line.

Mommy

M

Welcome to Critterville! Meet some more critters who live and work in Critterville. Use the word bank to label the critters with their correct names. Make sure their names and titles of respect start with capital letters.

Write two sentences about the folks in Critterville. Here is an example:

Mrs. Molini works at Molini's Market.

1. Mrs. Stork works at stork's Toys.

2. Mr. Rubble works at Rubble's Junk Yard.

Mommy

Review: Capitalization

Rewrite each red sentence correctly using the tips to help you.

Use a capital letter to begin a sentence.

this sentence starts with a capital letter.

The word **I** is always a capital letter.

i always try to do my best work.

A person's name or a pet's name always begins with a capital letter.

little critter has a dog named blue.

Miss, Mrs., Ms., and Mr. should begin with a capital letter.

miss Kitty is a great teacher.

Read Gabby's sentences below. Use this mark ≡ to show the letters that should be capitalized. Write the capital letter above each one.

1. M maurice and M molly love to read books.

2. M mr. and M mrs. C critter help out in M miss K kitty's class.

Read the paragraph below. Write this mark ≡ under the letters that should be capitalized. Write the capital letter above each one.

little sister and i have a lot of fun together. we go to the park almost every day in the summer. i like to look for frogs. little sister likes to climb on the monkey bars. when grandma and grandpa come to visit, they go to the park with us. we usually pack a picnic lunch to take along. Sometimes we see ms. greene, the park ranger. she does a great job taking care of the park. i once gave her a cookie to thank her.

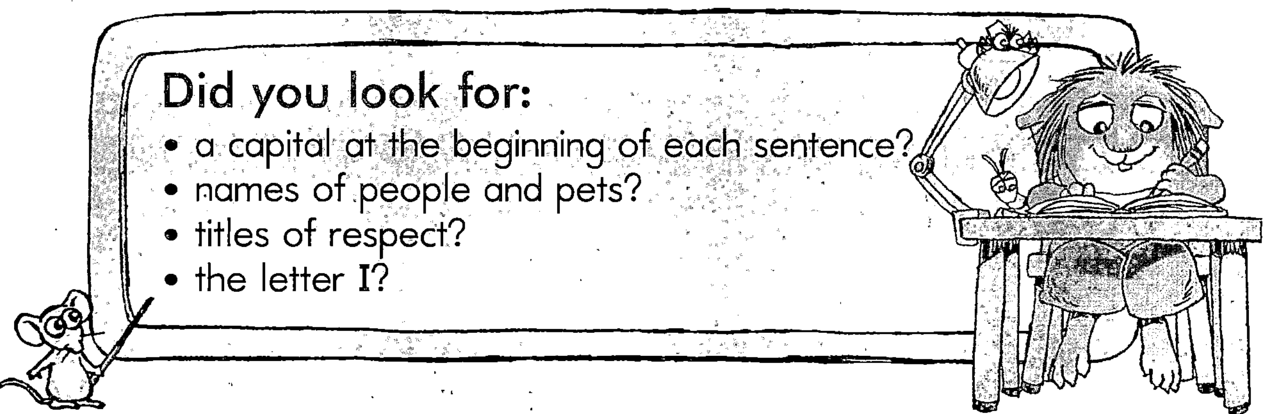

Did you look for:

- a capital at the beginning of each sentence?
- names of people and pets?
- titles of respect?
- the letter I?

Places

There are many kinds of places. Use a capital letter for the first letter of the name of each special place.

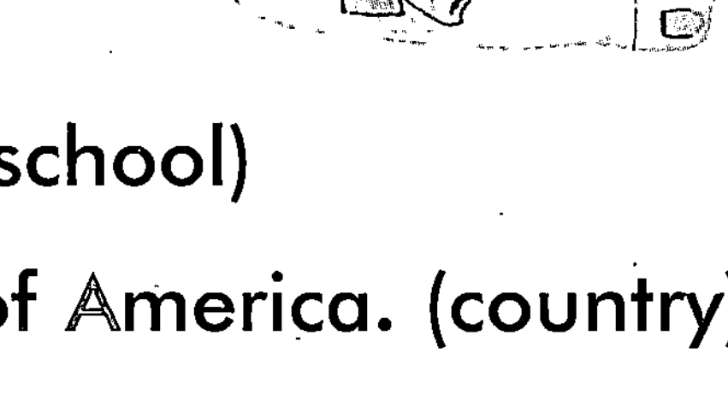

Tiger visited the Critterville Zoo. (zoo)

Gator is from North Carolina. (state)

Gabby stayed overnight in Orlando. (city)

Bun Bun lives on Sweet Street. (street)

Little Critter goes to Critterville School. (school)

Malcolm was born in the United States of America. (country)

Learn about Critterville. Use this mark ≡ to show the letters that should be capitalized. Write the capital letter above each one. See if you can find all nine words that need to be corrected.

Ms. Dingo is from australia.

The junkyard is on treasure street.

The critterville zoo is a fun place to visit.

Mr. Stork used to live in new york city.

Miss Kitty was born in michigan.

Ms. Dingo

Miss Kitty

Fill in the blanks below. Don't forget to use capital letters.

I live in thy United States of America.
(name of country)

I live in New Jersey.
(name of state)

I live in Cherry Hill.
(name of city)

I live on 112 Sunny brook Rd.
(name of street)

I go to My home.
(name of school)

Read Gabby's book report. Use this mark ≡ to show the words that should be capitalized. Write the capital letter above each one.

I read a mystery that took place in the united states of america. The detective finds the first clue on mt. wilson in california. She finds the second clue beside lake okeechobee in florida. She solves the mystery on elm street in her own backyard.

Days and Months

There are seven days in a week and 12 months in a year. These words always begin with a capital letter.

Days
Sunday
Monday
Tuesday
Wednesday
Thursday
Friday
Saturday

Months

January	July
February	August
March	September
April	October
May	November
June	December

The names of the months are all scrambled. Unscramble the letters and rewrite the months using a capital letter at the beginning of each month.

1. ujyarna	January	7. amy	May
2. yulj	July	8. rbonmeve	November
3. teroocb	October	9. embespter	Septe mber
4. guatus	August	10. enju	June
5. lapir	April	11. mbdceere	December
6. ryerbuaf	Febraury	12. arcmh	March

Circle your favorite month. Write a sentence about why it is your favorite.

March, cose its my Bday!

June, cose the pool opens!!!!!!

Look at Little Critter's calendar. Fill in the missing days of the week.

August						
Sunday	Monday	Tuesday	Wednesday	Thursday	Friday	Saturday
			1	2	3	4 Birthday party
5	6	7 Last soccer game	8	9	10	11
12	13	14	15 Dentist 10:00	16	17	18
19	20	21	22	23	24 Pool closes	25
26	27 First day of school	28	29	30	31	

Now use the calendar to fill in the blanks with the correct day of the week.
Example: The first day of school is on a Monday.

1. The Critterville Pool closes for the summer on a

Friday

2. Little Critter is going to a party on a

Saturday

3. Little Critter is going to the dentist on a

Wednesday

4. The last soccer game is on a

Tuesday

Friendly Letters

1) Date:
Begin with a date at the top. Always use a capital letter for the name of the month.

2) Greeting:
Start your greeting with **Dear.** Then write your friend's name. Begin each word with a capital letter.

3) Body:
The body of a letter is what you want to tell your friend. Use capital letters to begin each sentence.

4) Closing:
End the letter with a closing and your name. Use a capital letter to begin the closing. Your name should start with a capital letter, too.

August 31, 2001

Dear Friend,

My name is Little Critter. I have a younger sister. She is two years younger than I am. My friends' names are Gator, Gabby, Bun Bun, Tiger, Maurice, and Molly. I live with my mom and dad. My teacher's name is Miss Kitty. She makes school a lot of fun. I like to play baseball and ride my bike. This summer I went camping with my dad. Please write back and tell me about yourself.

Sincerely,
Little Critter

Now it is your turn. Write a letter back to Little Critter. Tell him at least three things about yourself. Don't forget to use capital letters.

February 9, 2004
Date

Dear Friend,
Greeting

→ My name is Olivia. I am home schooled. I have "3" sisters named, Corinne, Isabel, and Amealiea.

From,
Closing

Olivia Perham
(your name)

Editing Checklist:

I used capital letters for the:

- [x] date
- [x] greeting
- [x] beginning of a sentence
- [x] closing
- [x] names
- [x] the word I

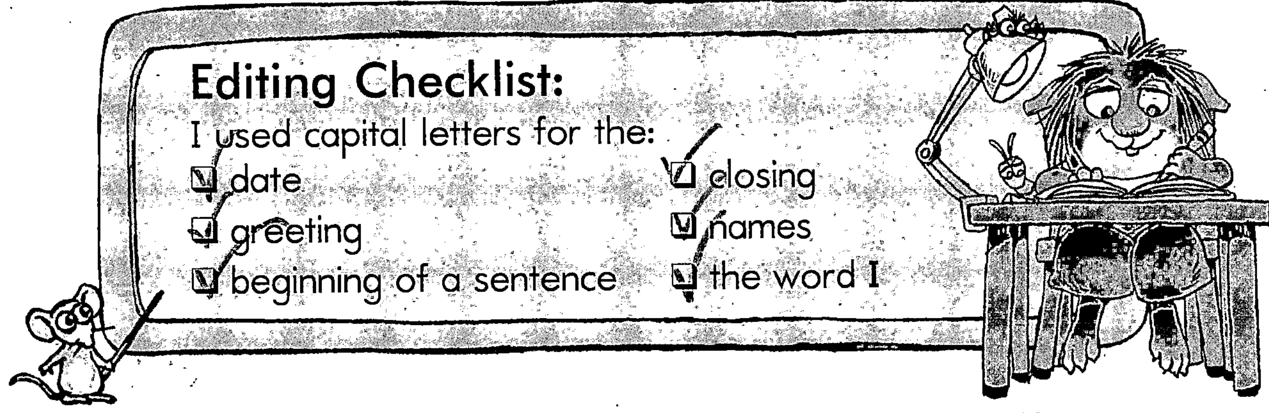

Review: Capitalization

Rewrite each red sentence correctly using the tips to help you.

Use a capital letter for the days of the week and the months of the year.

july 4th is Independence Day.

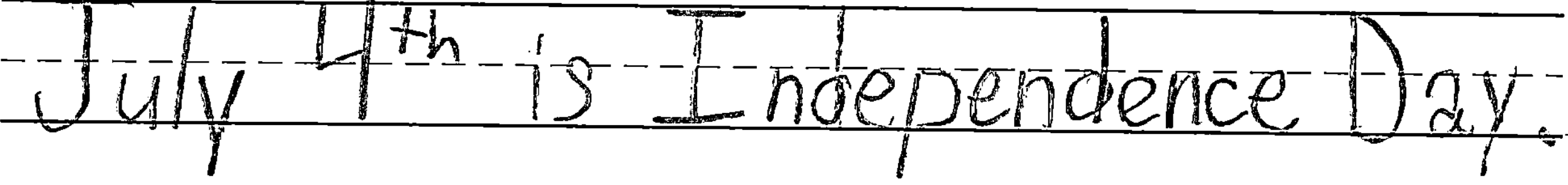

July 4th is Independence Day.

Use a capital letter for the names of cities or towns.

critterville is a great place to live.

Critterville is a great place to live.

Use a capital letter in the dates, greetings, and closings of friendly letters.

july 5, 2002

dear grandma,

Thanks for taking me to the fireworks. It was fun.

love,

little critter

July 5, 2002

Dear grandma

Thanks for taking me to the fireworks. It was fun.

love

Little Critter

Gator wrote a letter at camp. Use this mark ≡ to show where he needs capital letters. Write the capital letter above each mark.

J
july 31, 2001
≡

dear Little Critter,

today is tuesday. camp Critter is really neat. all the bugs are very big. i have a spider named fuzzy. her legs have a lot of hair. i put her in a jar on monday. spike is my snake. he sleeps with me in my sleeping bag. kyle, our camp leader, doesn't know about spike. i will show you spike and fuzzy when I come home in august. i cannot wait to see what I will find tomorrow!

sincerely,

gator

Did you look for a capital at the beginning of:

- each sentence?
- names of special places?
- the word I?
- names of people and pets?
- the date, greeting, and closing?
- days of the week and months of the year?

Complete Thoughts

A sentence tells a complete thought.

This is a sentence, because it is a complete thought.

Little Critter is excited about his birthday.

This is not a sentence, because it does not tell a complete thought.

A birthday cake.

Circle each group of words that forms a complete thought.

- Little Critter went into the house.
- It was quiet.
- Into the living room.
- He turned on the light.
- A surprise.
- Everyone popped out from behind the furniture.
- Laughing hard.

Subjects and Verbs

Every sentence has two parts, the naming part and the telling part. The naming part of a sentence tells who or what the sentence is about. The naming part is also called the subject of the sentence.

Tiger hid behind the couch.
The room was dark.

To Do: Look at your circled sentences on page 24. Underline the naming part or subject of each sentence.

The telling part of a sentence tells what someone or something is or does. The telling part of a sentence is also called the verb.

Tiger hid behind the couch.
The room was dark.

To Do: Look at your circled sentences on page 24 again. Use two lines to underline the verbs in your circled sentences.

Write a verb for each sentence. Then circle the subject(s) or naming part(s) in each sentence.

Gator and Tiger ____________, "Surprise!"

Everyone ____________ "Happy Birthday."

Little Critter ____________ a great birthday.

Periods

A period is like a stop sign. It tells the reader that a sentence has ended.

Little Critter likes to eat at Critterville Diner.

He always orders spaghetti with meatballs.

Put this mark ⊙ at the end of each sentence.

Little Sister likes apple pie with ice cream ⊙ Dad loves cheese and crackers ⊙ Bun Bun has carrots for a snack when she gets home from school ⊙ Grandma Critter likes to make vegetable soup ⊙ Mom and Little Critter enjoy juicy watermelon on hot summer days ⊙ Miss Kitty always has a cookie and a glass of milk when the school day is done ⊙

Read the story below. Five periods are missing. Use this mark ⊙ to add periods where they belong.

Little Critter was hungry⊙ He decided to make his favorite sandwich. First, he got two slices of bread⊙ Then, he spread some peanut butter on them. Next, he put on some pickles⊙ Finally, he added potato chips and orange juice. Little Criter took a bite⊙ His sandwich was delicious⊙

Write two sentences that tell something about a food you like. End each sentence with a period.

1. I like ice cream becose it has suger.

2. Oh and so, so, so, so, good.

A sentence tells a complete thought. There are four different kinds of sentences. They are: statements, questions, exclamations, and commands.

Four Kinds of Sentences:

- Statements
- Questions
- Exclamations
- Commands

Statements

A statement is a sentence that tells about something. Its first word begins with a capital letter. Use a period to end a sentence that tells about something.

Maurice is holding his picture.

Molly is reading a story.

Here are some statements about Maurice and Molly. Use these marks ≡ and ⊙ to show that the statements start with a capital letter and end with a period.

★maurice and Molly are twins

★molly is two minutes and twenty seconds older than maurice

★molly likes to write about butterflies

★maurice likes to draw pictures of dolphins

Maurice and Molly wrote some statements. Rewrite them using capital letters and periods correctly. Try to decide who wrote each statement. Check the box to show your guess.

Statement	Maurice	Molly
dolphins play games in the water	☐	☑

Dolphins play games in the water.

Statement	Maurice	Molly
a butterfly is a grown-up caterpillar	☐	☑

A butterfly is a grown-up.

Statement	Maurice	Molly
it is fun to have a brother	☐	☑

It is fun to have a brother.

Statement	Maurice	Molly
i am older	☐	☑

I am older.

Statement	Maurice	Molly
my twin sister wrote a story	☑	☐

My twin sister wrote a story.

Write two statements about yourself.

1. I am $7\frac{1}{2}$ years old 3 my
2.

Questions

All questions need me.
What am I?
I am a question mark.

A question is a sentence that asks something. Its first word begins with a capital letter. The sentence ends with a question mark.

What will I be when I grow up?

Taller.

Little Critter wants to find out more about you. Put a question mark ? at the end of each question, then answer the questions.

How old are you ? 7½

What is your favorite food? I do not Know!

Where do you live? Cherry Hill, N.J.

When is your birthday ? March 20th

What is your favorite sport? Swiming

What is your favorite season ? Summur 3 Spring

What is your favorite thing about school? nothing

> You can write a letter to Little Critter on his Web site. Tell him all about yourself. His Web address is:
>
> http://www.littlecritter.com/write_letter.html

Bat Child forgot to use question marks. Put them in the places where they belong.

Knock, knock.

Who's there

Owl.

Owl who

Owl you know unless you open the door

Knock, knock.

Who's there

Max.

Max who

Max no difference. Just open the door.

Knock, knock.

Who's there

Police.

Police who

Police let me in. It's cold out here.

Challenge: Look for question marks in books you read. Make a list of words that you often find at the beginning of questions.

Exclamations

An exclamation is a sentence that shows surprise or excitement. Its first word begins with a capital letter. The sentence ends with an exclamation point.

Oh, no!

A shark!

Read the poem below. Find three sentences where you could change the period to an exclamation point because the sentence shows surprise or excitement.

I swam around. The sea was calm.
My boat was right nearby.
And then I saw a fin I knew.
A shark was close. Oh, my.

I saw his teeth, his rows of teeth.
His jaws were quite a sight.
And he was coming straight for me.
I was his next big bite.

I swam so fast, I reached my boat.
I landed dripping wet.
And then my mom called from the hall,
"Are you done with your bath yet?"

Uh, oh! Little Critter used too many exclamation points. Read the poem and decide where he should have used a period instead. Cross out each unnecessary exclamation point and put this mark ⊙ in its place.

My dad and I went hiking!
We hiked from here to there!
We tramped along the trail!
And then we saw a bear!

The bear was picking berries!
I liked that furry beast!
But since the bear was going west,
My dad and I went east!

Now reread the poem. Practice reading exclamation points. Add excitement to your voice when you come to an exclamation point at the end of a sentence.

Write two exciting sentences about swimming. Be sure to end each with an exclamation point.

1. I love, love, love swimming!

2. We have a water slide at our pool!

Exclamation points are like periods that explode with excitement! Be careful not to use them too much. Save them for something really exciting.

Commands

A command is a sentence that gives directions or orders. Its first word begins with a capital letter. The sentence ends with a period or an exclamation point.

The Coach said, "Run five warm up laps. Then do twenty jumping jacks. Okay, go!"

Read the conversations below. Underline all of the commands.

Dad was giving Little Critter tips on how to play checkers. "Think two or three moves ahead. Set up your jumps. Be a good sport."

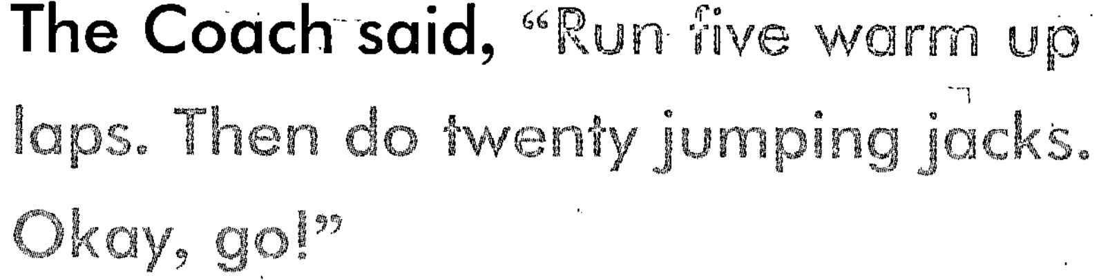

Little Critter's class went apple picking. Miss Kitty taught her students how to make applesauce. "First get permission and help from your parents. Wash your hands. Then peel and cut up your apples. Put the apples in a pan. Add sugar and cinnamon. Let them cook until they are soft. Mash up the cooked apples. Let the mixture cool before you eat it."

Write three command sentences that a coach, a teacher, or a parent might say.

1. Olivia, go to your room!

2. Corinne, set the table please.

3. Now, team, run, run, run, run, run!

Handwriting Check

Look at your handwriting above. Are your words sitting on the line? Did you take your time and use your best handwriting? Did you put spaces between your words? Do your tall letters touch the top line and your small letters fit between the dotted and the lower lines?

How did you do? (circle one)

Great! Good! O.K. I'll do better next time.

Review: Sentences and Punctuation

Read the story below carefully. Underline the three statements. Draw a circle around the question. Draw two lines under the two exclamations. Draw a box around the command. Add the proper marks at the end of each sentence.

The snow fell all night Today is a snow day Let's go sledding down Critterville Hill I will bring my sled Can you bring your inner tube Great We will have lots of fun

Read the poem below. Put a period after six statements. Put a question mark after one question. Put an exclamation point after one exciting statement.

I was building a snowman in my yard
Finding the snow was not too hard
A big, big snowstorm came last night
Everything here was covered in white

The snowball I made started to roll
It picked up speed and went out of control
It got bigger and bigger on its way down
Where would it stop when it rolled into town

Read each sentence below. Decide whether it is a question, an exclamation, a command, or a statement. Circle the correct answer.

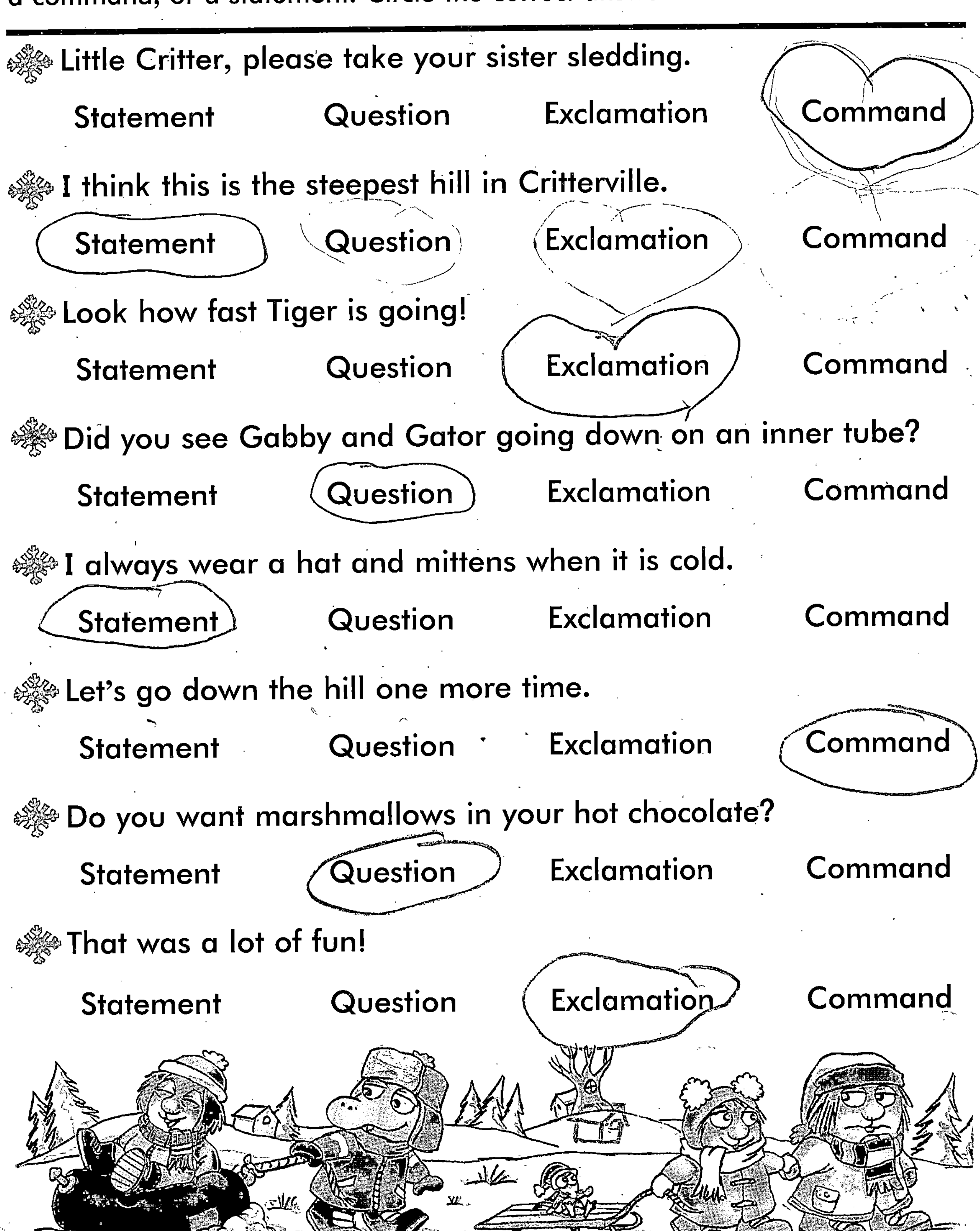

Little Critter, please take your sister sledding.

Statement   Question   Exclamation   Command

I think this is the steepest hill in Critterville.

Statement   Question   Exclamation   Command

Look how fast Tiger is going!

Statement   Question   Exclamation   Command

Did you see Gabby and Gator going down on an inner tube?

Statement   Question   Exclamation   Command

I always wear a hat and mittens when it is cold.

Statement   Question   Exclamation   Command

Let's go down the hill one more time.

Statement   Question   Exclamation   Command

Do you want marshmallows in your hot chocolate?

Statement   Question   Exclamation   Command

That was a lot of fun!

Statement   Question   Exclamation   Command

Cities and States

A comma goes between the name of a city and a state.

Columbus, Ohio

New York, New York

Denver, Colorado

Help Little Critter label these cities and states. The city names are in blue and the state names are in red. Write the city and state on the line. Place a comma between the name of the city and the state. Remember to use a capital letter at the beginning of the name of a city or state.

Columbus, Ohio

Dallas, Texas

Orlando, Florida

Juneau, Alaska

Fill in the blank with a city and state.

I live in Cherry Hill, New Jersey.

Someday I would like to visit Laguna Miguel, Ca.

I know someone who lives in Laguna Miguel, Ca.

Add six commas where they are needed. Use this proofreader's mark ^.

Miss Kitty's class was studying funny names of cities in the United States. The students read about Boulder Colorado. They wondered if the rocks in that city are bigger than the rocks in Little Rock Arkansas. Do ghosts really live in Casper Wyoming? Does everyone sew in Needles California? The class decided that there must be a lot of bookstores in Reading Pennsylvania. And they wondered if any aliens live in Neptune Ohio.

Challenge: Use a map or an atlas to see if you can find more cities with funny names.

Commas in Friendly Letters

1) Date:
Whenever you write a date, put a comma between the day and the year.

2) Greeting:
Put a comma after the greeting.

3) Closing:
A comma goes after the closing.

June 26, 2001

Dear Grandma,

I can't wait to go to the beach with you. Will you teach me how to surf?

Sincerely,
Little Critter

Add three commas to Grandma's letter. Use this proofreader's mark ^.

July 2 2001

Dear Little Critter

Since I don't know how to surf, I can't teach you, but I can show you how to build a sandcastle. I am looking forward to your visit. See you soon.

Sincerely
Grandma

Pretend you are Little Critter. Write a letter to your mom and dad telling them all about your day at the beach with Grandma. Don't forget to use commas.

July 6, 2001
Date

Dear Mom 3 Dad,
Greeting

With Grandma I made sandcastles, and got bit by a crab! And we played Jumping Jelly fish! It was a sunny and I got a Larg icecream cone! And got sunburned!!

Love,
Closing

Little Critter

Commas in Lists

A comma goes between each person, place, thing, or phrase in a list.

Grandma has a wonderful garden. She grows beans, tomatoes, onions, and peppers.

Read each sentence below. Make the lists in the sentences easier to read by putting nine commas where they are needed. Use this proofreader's mark ^, .

1. Little Critter has a dog a cat a fish and a frog.

2. Miss Kitty called on Maurice Molly Gabby and Gator during math class.

3. Little Critter likes peanut butter pickles potato chips and orange juice on his sandwich.

Make a list of your three favorite foods and three favorite toys in the boxes below.

Foods:	Toys:

Write one sentence that lists your favorite foods. Write another sentence that lists your favorite toys. Use commas in your sentences.

1.

2.

Review: Commas

Read Gabby's story about Gabbilocks. Add five commas where they are needed.

Gabbilocks and the Three Bears

Gabbilocks was lost in the woods. She came to a house and went in. She thought that the three bowls of porridge were too hot too cold and just right. She thought that the three chairs were too hard too soft and just right. She found a bed and fell asleep. The bear family came home. Gabbilocks woke up and ran away. Then Gabbilocks visited her grandma in Honeyville Maine. Grandma told her to write a letter to the bear family.

Add the commas in Gabbilocks' letter. Use this proofreader's mark ^, .

June 10 2001

Dear Bear Family

I got lost in the woods. I went to your house because I was scared. I am sorry that I ate sat and slept in your house. Will you visit me in Honeyville Maine? We have lots of fruit nuts and honey.

Sincerely
Gabbilocks

Read the sentences below. Use this proofreader's mark ^ to add fourteen commas where they belong.

On August 10 2001, Papa Bear Mama Bear and Baby Bear left the woods in a plane. They landed in Honeyville Maine.

Gabbilocks met them at the airport. She was so pleased that they had come to visit her and her grandma.

At Grandma's house, they ate apples oranges berries nuts and pears. Gabbilocks gave Baby Bear a new chair. She made yellow green and blue cushions for Mama Bear and Papa Bear.

On August 12 2001, the Bears had to return to Woods Pennsylvania. The Bears thanked Gabbilocks and Grandma for all the food fun and presents. They also gave Gabbilocks a key to their house and invited her to come over whenever she wants.

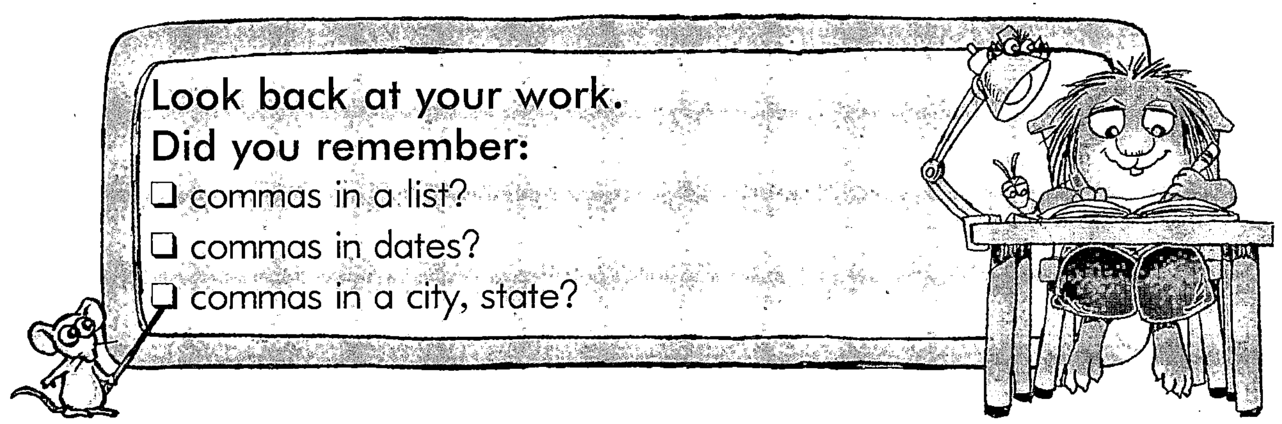

Quotation Marks in Dialogue

Quotation marks go before and after a speaker's words. Little Sister says, "Use quotation marks around words that someone says aloud."

Read Little Sister's silly sentences below. Circle each speaker's exact words.

1. Does anybody have some glue? asked Humpty Dumpty.

2. We are so hungry, we could eat a house! said Hansel and Gretel.

3. Prince Charming told Cinderella, If the shoe fits, wear it.

4. Don't wolf down your food! exclaimed Little Red Riding Hood.

5. The White Rabbit said, Digital watches are best.

6. The woman who swallowed a fly said, Yuck!

Finish the sentences below. Use the words from the cartoon. Remember to use quotation marks before and after a speaker's words.

Will you teach me how to steal a base?

Sure, but you have to promise to give it back.

Little Critter asked, "Will you teach me how to steal a base?"

Tiger replied, "______________________________

______________________________"

What's worse than finding a worm in an apple?

Finding half a worm.

Little Critter asked, ______________________________

____

Dad replied, ______________________________

____

Periods in Abbreviations

Some words can be made shorter or abbreviated. Abbreviations end with a period. Days of the week and months of the year can be abbreviated only when used in a date.

Examples:

Saturday, August 4, 2001 → Sat., Aug. 4, 2001

Monday, April 1, 2002 → Mon., Apr. 1, 2002

Days of the Week: Match the day of the week to the correct abbreviation.

Sunday	Thurs.
Monday	Sun.
Tuesday	Wed.
Wednesday	Mon.
Thursday	Fri.
Friday	Sat.
Saturday	Tues.

Months of the Year: Circle the abbreviations. Write the abbreviated word next to each month using a period. Hint: Use the first 3 letters of the month. For September, use the first four letters. May, June, and July are already short enough!

January	Jan.
February	______
March	______
April	______
August	______
September	______
October	______
November	______
December	______

Abbreviate the dates below. Don't forget to use a period in each abbreviated word. Also, use capital letters where they belong.

thursday, september 13, 2001 → Thurs., Sept. 13, 2001

wednesday, november 7, 2001 → ____________

monday, february 18, 2002 → ____________

saturday, august 17, 2002 → ____________

tuesday, january 22, 2001 → ____________

friday, april 19, 2002 → ____________

sunday, may 6, 2001 → ____________

There is an even shorter way to write dates. Use numbers! 8/4/01 means August 4, 2001. The months of the year, beginning with January are numbered 1 to 12. Number the months on the left. Then try the shortest way to write the dates below.

____ January
____ February
____ March
____ April
____ May
____ June
____ July
____ August
____ September
____ October
____ November
____ December

Aug. 16, 2001 → 8/16/01

Oct. 31, 2001 → ____________

Dec. 25, 2001 → ____________

Mar. 4, 2002 → ____________

Apostrophes in Possessives

An apostrophe followed by an **s** is used to show that someone owns something. Just add an apostrophe when the owner's name ends with an **s.**

Tiger's team is playing Malcolm's team.

Note: When two or more people own something you just add an apostrophe.

All of the players' bats are made of wood.

Add 's to each critter's name to show that he or she owns something.

Little Critter hat

Malcolm lunchbox

Gator backpack

Gabby book

Label the pictures below. Look at page 4 to help you spell the names.

Use the pictures above and on page 50 to help you write two sentences to show ownership. Don't forget to use 's in each sentence.

Example: Tiger's shoe is blue.

1.

2.

Handwriting Check

Look at your handwriting above. Are your words sitting on the line? Did you take your time and use your best handwriting? Did you put spaces between your words? Do your tall letters touch the top line and your small letters fit between the dotted and the lower lines?

How did you do? (circle one)

Great!

Good!

O.K.

I'll do better next time.

Underlining Titles

Underline the titles of books and movies when you are writing their names. Think of the line as a shelf and pretend you are putting the book on a shelf.

Little Critter loves to visit the library. His favorite books are The Wizard of Oz and Just So Stories.

Read each sentence below. Underline each title.

1. Bat Child is reading 101 Knock-Knock Jokes to Amuse Your Friends.

2. The Carrot Seed is Bun Bun's favorite book.

3. Maurice and Molly just finished reading Double Trouble.

4. In the spring Grandma Critter read Grow Your Own Vegetable Soup.

Read each sentence below. Underline the four book and movie titles.

1. After Little Sister read Peter Pan, she wished she could fly to Never-Never Land.

2. Little Critter and his friends went to see the movie The Further Adventures of Super Critter ten times.

3. Gabby gave Gator the book Treasure Island for his birthday.

4. Molly said that The Wind in the Willows is her favorite book.

Write two sentences about your favorite book and movie. Don't forget to underline the titles.

1. ______________________________

2. ______________________________

Challenge: Make a list of all the books you read in one month. Record the titles in a notebook. Remember to underline the titles. Next month, try to read even more books!

Review: Punctuation

Read the story below. Circle the set of words in the sentences where quotation marks should be used.

Little Critter asked, Mom, can I take the recycling down to the market? Sure, That would be a big help, replied Mom. Little Critter stopped to get the mail on his way out. Hey Mom! I got a letter, he yelled.

Who is it from? asked Mom.

It is an invitation to a costume party.

Yippee! yelled Little Critter.

Maybe you can look for costume ideas when you are in town, said Dad.

That is a great idea. Bye! said Little Critter.

Write the abbreviations.

Please come to my costume party!

When: 3:00 on ________ (Saturday), ________ (October) 27th

Where: 26 Critterville ________ (Street)

Read the following paragraph. Find book titles and underline them.

Little Critter stopped by Gator's house on the way into town. Gator had received an invitation from Gabby, too. They decided to go to the library to get some books about costumes. Gator checked out Creative Costumes. Little Critter checked out Fabulous Costumes Without Sewing and Crazy Costumes You Can Make. Then they headed to the market.

Show ownership by adding an apostrophe and an s ('s) to a name. Write the names so that they show ownership.

Little Critter and Gator walked to ____________ (Mr. Molini) Market. They walked past ____________ (Hogley) Hardware. After they dropped the recycling off at the market, they decided to take the long way home. They walked past the pet store, the pond, and the zoo. Little Critter bought a yo-yo at ____________ (Stork) Toy Shop. He tried it out as they walked to ____________ (Mrs. Castle) Costume Shop. Inside they found some great costume ideas for ____________ (Gabby) party. Finally, they headed home. They were ready to make their costumes. What do you think they decided to be? ____________________________

Verbs – Has, Have

A verb is a word that tells what the subject of the sentence does.

Use has when you are talking about one subject.

Little Sister has a shadow.

Use have when you are talking about yourself or more than one subject.

I have a shadow.
My friends have shadows, too.

Little Sister wrote a story about her shadow. Read the sentences below. Fill in each blank with **has** or **have**.

I ____________ a shy shadow. I think it ____________ a hiding place. It also ____________ many shapes. I ____________ only one shape. My shadow and I ____________ a good time together.

This letter has five mistakes. Draw a line through each incorrect word. Write the correct word above it. When you are done, read the letter aloud to be sure it makes sense.

have

Example: The teams ~~has~~ colorful uniforms.

May 10, 2001

Dear Grandma,

I am on a t-ball team. It have 10 players. Our uniforms are cool. We have red shirts and white pants. The red shirts has blue numbers on them. Mine have a number 6 on it. We has a game on Saturday. I has butterflies in my stomach. Wish me luck.

Love,

Little Sister

Write one sentence about something you have. Write another sentence about something a friend has.

1. ______________________________

2. ______________________________

Verbs – Is, Are

Is and are are verbs. They tell what the subject of the sentence is.

Use is when you are talking about one subject.

Malcolm is always doing something funny.

Use are when you are talking about more than one subject.

Little Critter and Gabby are funny, too.

Read the sentences below. Fill in each blank with **is** or **are**.

Little Critter and Gabby ________ being silly.

So ________ Malcolm. He ________ acting like a creature from outer space. They ________ all waiting for the bus. I think it ________ time for the bus to come.

This paragraph has six mistakes. Draw a line through each incorrect word. Write the correct word above it. When you are done, read the sentences aloud to be sure they make sense.

Example: The children ~~is~~ are in the park.

Tiger and Gator is at the park. They is waiting for their friends. Little Critter are coming on the bus. Gabby and Malcolm is coming with him. Tiger are looking down the street. He sees the bus two blocks away. His friends is on their way.

Write one sentence about your friend. Write another sentence about the two of you. Use **is** in one sentence and **are** in the other one.

1. ______________________________

2. ______________________________

Verbs – Was, Were

Was and were are used to tell something that happened in the past. Note: Use were with the word you.

Use was when you are talking about one person.

Little Critter was hurrying to school.

Use were when you are talking about more than one person or thing.

They were hurrying to school.

Fill in the blanks with **was** or **were**.

Little Critter ________ in a hurry. He had to go back home and get his lunchbox. Maurice and Molly ________ in a hurry, too. They overslept and ________ late. It ________ not a good way to start the day. Luckily, they made it to school on time. They ________ not late.

This story has four mistakes. Draw a line through each incorrect word. Write the correct word above it.

Example: We ~~was~~ were on time.

Malcolm was in the lunchroom. His lunch were at home on the kitchen counter. His grandma were at work. Malcolm were hungry. Little Critter shared his lunch. Then Malcolm were not hungry anymore.

Write two sentences telling about what happened when you forgot something. Use **was** or **were** in each sentence.

1. ______________________________

____

2. ______________________________

____

Handwriting Check

Look at your handwriting above. Are your words sitting on the line? Did you take your time and use your best handwriting? Did you put spaces between your words? Do your tall letters touch the top line and your small letters fit between the dotted and the lower lines?

How did you do? (circle one)

Great!

Good!

O.K.

I'll do better next time.

Verbs – Ran, Run

Ran and run are forms of the verb to run.

Use ran alone.

> I ran as fast as I could.
> My dog ran behind me.

Use run with has or have.

> I have run with my dog.
> Blue has run along with me.

Read the sentences. Write **ran** or **run** in each blank.

☆Tiger has ________ many races.

☆Little Critter and Gator have ________ many races with him.

☆Tiger ________ faster than everybody else.

☆Tiger ________ faster than the wind.

There are five mistakes in this paragraph. Draw a line through each incorrect word. Write the correct word above it.

run
Example: The boy has ~~ran~~ after the ball.

Gator run across the basketball court. Tiger and Gabby run to block him. They have ran to block him before. But Gator is a good basketball player. He throws the ball. It goes through the hoop. Now Little Critter has ran onto the court. He will take Gator's place. Gator has ran enough for a while.

Think about animals, people, and things that run. Write one sentence using **ran**. Write another using **has run** or **have run**.

1. ____

____

2. ____

____

Challenge: Clocks run, fans run, and children run to have fun! Make a list of all the things that run. Walk around the house to help you come up with ideas.

Review: Verbs

Read the sentences. Write **is** or **are** in each blank.

It ________ fall. Little Critter and Little Sister ________ happy. They ________ going to pick apples. It ________ fun. It ________ also hard work, because the apples ________ heavy.

Read the sentences. Write **was** or **were** in each blank.

The leaves ________ all over the yard. Little Critter raked them into a big pile. Little Sister ________ there. She ________ helping. When Little Critter finished, they ran toward the pile. The pile ________ high. Little Critter and Little Sister jumped in the leaves.

Read this paragraph. Look for **has** and **have**. If the word is used incorrectly, draw a line through it. Write the correct word above it.

I has four apples. Little Sister have three apples. Together we have enough to make a pie. Mom have a good recipe for apple pie. We has fun making a yummy dessert for dinner.

Read the sentences below. If the underlined word is incorrect, draw a line through it. Write the correct word above it.

Grandpa has an old clock in the hall. It has ran for a hundred years. He has a car and a tractor. They have ran for thirty years. He has a dog and a cat. They have ran for ten years. The dog ran after the cat. The cat run after a mouse and the mouse run up the clock.

Verbs – Did, Done

Did and done are forms of the verb to do.

Use did alone.

I did my homework.
Gator did his, too.

Use done with has or have.

I have done all my homework.
Gator has done his, too.

Gator made a list of all the things he accomplished this week. Review his list below. If the underlined word is used incorrectly, draw a line through it. Write the correct word above it.

- ❑ I <u>did</u> the dishes.
- ❑ I <u>done</u> the yard work.
- ❑ I have <u>did</u> the vacuuming.
- ❑ I have <u>done</u> my laundry.
- ❑ I <u>done</u> my paper route.

"All of my chores have been <u>did</u>. I have <u>did</u> a lot this week!" exclaimed Gator.

This report has four mistakes. Draw a line through each incorrect word. Write the correct word above it.

Example: We ~~done~~ did a good job.

The members of the Critterville Nature Club done something for their town. They cleaned up the park. They have did some hiking and exploring together, but this was different. They done a great job picking up litter. Gabby made a No Littering poster. Tiger and Little Critter painted the trash cans. The Nature Club has did a lot of good things to make Critterville Park a nice place.

Think about a chore you or your friends have done. Write two sentences about it. Be sure to use **did**, **have done**, or **has done** in each sentence.

1. ______________________________

____

2. ______________________________

____

Verbs – Went, Gone

Went and gone are forms of the verb to go.

Use went alone.

Malcolm went to the carnival.

Use gone with has or have.

Little Critter has gone to the carnival, too.

Read the sentences. Write **went** or **gone** in each blank.

Little Critter __________ to the carnival. His family has __________ every year. First, he __________ in the Fun House. Next he __________ on the Ferris Wheel. Then he __________ on all the other rides. He and his sister have __________ on all the rides before, but they love to go again and again.

This paragraph has four mistakes. Draw a line through each incorrect word. Write the correct word above it.

gone

Example: My sister has ~~went~~ to school.

Dad and I went to a soccer game. Gabby has went with us. We have went to pick up Gator and Tiger. Malcolm has went ahead. He has went to buy tickets. His grandma went with him.

Write two sentences about a time you went somewhere. Be sure to use **went**, **has gone**, or **have gone** in each sentence.

1. ______________________________

2. ______________________________

Verbs – Saw, Seen

Saw and seen are forms of the verb to see.

Use saw alone.

I saw a picture of the Grand Canyon.

Use seen with has or have.

Dad has seen the Grand Canyon in real life.

Read the sentences. Write **saw** or **seen** in each blank.

The Critter family was going on a trip. Little Critter and Little Sister were very excited because they had never __________ the Grand Canyon before. On the way they __________ a sign for the World's Largest Ball of String. They also __________ a lot of corn fields. They drove for hours and hours. "Has anyone __________ the map?" asked Dad. "Dad, I __________ a sign for the Grand Canyon. It is only 10 miles away," said Little Critter. "Good job, Little Critter," said Dad. Finally, they arrived at the Grand Canyon. "I have never __________ anything like it," said Little Critter.

Little Critter's postcard has two mistakes. Draw a line through each incorrect word. Write the correct word above it.

saw
Example: We ~~seen~~ a bear in the woods.

August 1, 2002

Dear Maurice and Molly,

We are having fun on our trip. I seen giant sequoia trees. They are taller than buildings. I never seen anything like them before. I wish you were here.

From,
Little Critter

Maurice and Molly
22 Foxtail Road
Critterville, U.S.A.

Write two sentences about something you have seen. Remember to use **saw**, **has seen**, or **have seen** in each sentence.

1. ______________________________

____

2. ______________________________

____

Verbs – Came, Come

Came and come are forms of the verb to come.

Use came alone.

Everyone came to Gabby's party in a costume.

Use come with has or have.
Use has come with one subject.

Bun Bun has come dressed as a ballerina.

Use have come when you talk about more then one subject.

Maurice and Molly have come dressed as a pair of mittens.

Fill in each blank with **came** or **come**.

- Little Critter __________ early to help Gabby set up.
- Malcolm has __________ dressed as a pirate.
- Gator and Tiger have __________ as storybook characters.
- Gabby is glad all of her friends __________ to the party.

After the party, Gabby wrote a note to Bun Bun. There are some mistakes in this letter. Draw a line through each incorrect word. Write the correct word above it.

November 1, 2001

Dear Bun Bun,

I am glad you come to my party. I have came to all of your parties. Thank you for bringing cookies. I didn't know you made them. I thought they come from the store.

Your friend,

Gabby

Note: **Come** can be used by itself when you are asking someone to come with you to a party or event.

Example: Please come to the library with me.

Write two sentences asking someone to come with you somewhere.

1. ______________________________

____

2. ______________________________

____

Review: Verbs

Read the sentences. Write **came** or **come** in each blank.

The sea __________ to the beach yesterday.

It has __________ again today.

Do you think it __________ to find a shell?

Maybe it has __________ with a tale to tell.

Read Little Critter's story below. Write **saw** or **seen** in each blank.

I went to the circus. I __________ a clown riding a mule. Then I noticed something funny. I __________ two monkeys riding on the clown. I have not __________ that before! Then I __________ dogs riding on each of the monkeys. Did you see eight fleas riding on each of the dogs?

Challenge: How many things were riding on the mule? Don't forget to count the monkeys, dogs, and fleas.

Read the story below. Choose the correct word and write it in the blank.

Little Sister has ________ (went, gone) to the park. She wants to climb on the monkey bars. Gabby and Little Critter ________ (went, gone) with her. They have ________ (went, gone) to slide and swing. Little Sister ________ (did, done) it. She climbed to the top of the monkey bars. Oh, no! What has she ________ (did, done)! She can't get down. Little Critter ________ (went, gone) to help her. He has ________ (did, done) a very nice thing. What a thoughtful big brother.

Look at the words in each column. Draw a line between pairs that make sense. Use each pair only once.

Maurice and Molly have	went to see the movie star.
My brother	ran to get the mail.
Gabby	gone to feed the ducks.
Little Sister has	come home early today.
Bat Child	run in a race.
I think Tiger has	came to the park with us.

Adjectives That Compare

We can use words to describe and compare things. Add -er to an adjective when you compare two things. Add -est when you compare three or more things.

Little Critter is **fast.**

Gabby is **faster.**

Tiger is the **fastest.**

This chart is not finished. Fill in the empty boxes with the correct word.

fast	faster	fastest
	shorter	shortest
large		largest
	brighter	
long	longer	
		highest

Tiger's report has four mistakes. Draw a line through each incorrect word. Write the correct word above it.

shorter
Example: Maurice is ~~shortest~~ than Tiger.

A gorilla is big. A chimp is smallest than a gorilla. A baboon is smart. A gorilla is smart than a baboon. Did you know that a baboon is a monkey, not an ape? Someone old than I am told me that. Apes are smarter than monkeys and chimps are the smarter of the apes.

Use the words from the chart on page 76 to compare something. Write two sentences. Be sure to write complete sentences, like the ones below.

Little Critter is taller than Little Sister.
Malcolm is the tallest boy in the class.

1. ______________________________

____

2. ______________________________

____

Homophones – To, Too, Two

Some words sound alike even when they mean different things and have different spellings. These words are called homophones.

The word to has two meanings. It can mean "toward." To is also used before a verb.

I found a penny when I walked to the store.
I want to read that book.

The word too has two meanings. It can mean "also." Too can also be used to mean "very" or "more than enough."

My brother found a penny, too.
I am too tired to watch the movie.

The word two means the number 2.

Bun Bun found two pennies.

Read Little Sister's paragraph below. Fill in each blank with **to**, **too**, or **two**.

My brother is learning __________ juggle. He started with __________ balls. I asked him __________ teach me, __________.

Little Critter's diary entry has four mistakes. Draw a line through each incorrect word. Write the correct word above it.

too
Example: I'm not ~~to~~ sleepy.

Maurice and Molly asked me to come too their house after school. They are going two have to kinds of snacks. Tiger is coming. Gabby isn't coming. She is to busy.

PRETZELS
CHIP

Write two sentences. One should be about two of something. The other should tell about going to a place you like. Try to use too in one of the sentences, too!

1. ______________________________

2. ______________________________

Challenge: Here are some other homophones. Read them to someone and talk about their different meanings. Can you think of any others?

one/won	sun/son	new/knew	for/four
your/you're	ate/eight	read/red	know/no
meet/meat	blew/blue	their/there/they're	

Review: Adjectives That Compare, Homophones

Fill in the empty boxes to complete the chart.

slow		
fast	faster	
	darker	
little		littlest
tall		
		shortest

Read the poem below. Write **to**, **too**, or **two** in each blank.

This morning it started ________ rain.

The ________ of us were sad.

We couldn't go ________ the soccer game.

"That's ________ bad," said Dad.

Finish the comparisons by writing the correct word in each blank.

1. Little Critter is ________________ than Little Sister.
   old, older, oldest

2. Little Sister is the ________________ member of the family.
   young, younger, youngest

3. Dad is ________________ than Mom.
   tall, taller, tallest

4. Mom's ice cream cone is the ________________.
   big, bigger, biggest

5. Little Critter's ice cream is melting the ________________.
   fast, faster, fastest

6. The sun is ________________.
   hot, hotter, hottest

Plurals That Add -s

Nouns are words that name objects. You can make most nouns mean "more than one" by adding -s to the end of the word. This is called a plural noun.

one shoe — two shoes
one ball — five balls

Write each word so that it means more than one.

1. animal animals
2. sister ______
3. kitten ______
4. truck ______
5. backpack ______
6. bat ______
7. book ______
8. toy ______
9. dog ______
10. river ______

Fill in each blank with the correct plural by adding **-s** or **-es** to the word below each line.

Maurice and Molly went to the Critterville Zoo. They saw

zebras (zebra) and ____________ (lion). They ate their ____________ (lunch) on a couple of ____________ (bench). In the petting zoo, they touched ____________ (snake), ____________ (goat) and baby ____________ (fox).

The seals made a lot of ____________ (splash). Wow! Did the ____________ (twin) get wet!

Choose two words that mean more than one from the list on page 84. Use each word in a sentence.

1. ____

2. ____

Review: Plurals

Add **-s** to make each word mean "more than one." Write the word on the line.

1. ball
2. bat
3. shoe
4. glove
5. field

Add **-es** to make each word mean "more than one." Write the word on the line.

1. brush
2. box
3. wish
4. mess
5. branch

Fill in the blanks by adding -s or -es to the word below each line.

1. Grandma sent me a box of ____________.
paint

2. She also sent two new ____________.
brush

3. My sister got ten ____________.
marker

4. We made a lot of ____________.
picture

5. We made a lot of ____________, too.
mess

6. I am sending two ____________ to Grandma.
painting

7. One is a boy holding two ____________ of flowers.
bunch

8. One is a girl and a boy on their ____________.
bike

Handwriting Check

Look at your handwriting above. Are your words sitting on the line? Did you take your time and use your best handwriting? Did you put spaces between your words? Do your tall letters touch the top line and your small letters fit between the dotted and the lower lines?

How did you do? (circle one)

Great! Good! O.K. I'll do better next time.

Contractions

Sometimes we put two words together to make one shorter word. The shorter word is called a contraction. An apostrophe (') is put in the place of the letters that are left out when two words are put together.

is not	=	isn't
are not	=	aren't
we will	=	we'll
they are	=	they're

Look at the words in the first column. Circle the correct contraction in the same row.

cannot	cann't	cant'	can't
it is	it's	itis	its'
did not	didn't	din't	didnt
I am	I'am	I'm	Im'
I will	Iw'll	I'll	Ill
we are	we'ere	w're	we're
you are	you're	y'ar	youer
I have	I'ave	I've	Ih've
she would	she'd	shewo'd	shel'l

Write the correct contraction in each blank.

1. Little Sister ________________ want to clean her room.
didn't, don't

2. Little Critter said ________________ help her.
he'd, she'd

3. "Maybe ________________ find my fishing pole, he told her.
I'll, I'm

4. "I ________________ have
didn't, don't

any of your stuff,"

said Little Sister.

Fill in the blanks with the correct contraction.

________________ helping Little Sister clean her room. First,
I am

________________ look in her closet. ________________ a real mess in
I will It is

there. I ________________ believe my eyes. Look at all this stuff
cannot

she borrowed from me. ________________ a feeling my
I have

fishing pole is in there, too.

Isn't, Aren't

Isn't and aren't are contractions.

Use isn't when you talk about one.

Little Critter isn't playing ball.

Use aren't when you talk about more than one.

Gabby and Tiger aren't playing ball, either.

Read the story below. Write **isn't** or **aren't** in the blanks.

Little Critter __________ eating his peas. He put them in the flowerpot. Mom saw him. Peas __________ part of her ivy plant. Then Little Critter tried to make Blue eat his peas. Blue __________ happy. I hope Little Critter's peas __________ about to land on my plate!

Read Gabby's paragraph about four animals she saw at the zoo. Draw a line through each incorrect word. Write the correct word above it. There are three mistakes.

isn't
Example: That book ~~aren~~'t about snakes.

Seals and sea lions can swim but they isn't fish. A bat can fly but it isnt a bird. An armadillo is covered with bony plates but it aren't a reptile. Seals, sea lions, bats, and armadillos are all mammals.

Write two sentences about animals that are different. Use **isn't** and **aren't**.

Example: Zebras and giraffes aren't the same.
A zebra isn't as tall as a giraffe.

1. ______________________________

____

2. ______________________________

____

Wasn't, Weren't

Wasn't and weren't are two more contractions.

Use wasn't when you talk about one.

Gabby wasn't at the clubhouse.

Use weren't when you talk about more than one and with the word you.

Tiger and Gator weren't at the clubhouse, either.
You weren't able to find them right away.

Read this paragraph that Little Critter's mom wrote about him. She left out the words **wasn't** and **weren't**. Write the correct word in each blank.

You were looking for your friends. They ______________ playing ball. Tiger ______________ at the karate school. Gabby ______________ at the library. Gator ______________ in his backyard. ______________ you surprised to find them at your house, looking for you?

Bun Bun's thank you note has three mistakes. Draw a line through each incorrect word. Write the correct word above it.

weren't
Example: You ~~wasn't~~ late.

Dear Mrs. Critter,

Thank you for taking me to the circus. Weren't it fun? I weren't really scared. I knew those two acrobats weren't going to fall. You wasn't scared, were you?

Love,

Bun Bun

Write two sentences. Use **wasn't** or **weren't** in each sentence.

Example: The car wasn't big.
The clowns weren't happy.

1. ______________________________

2. ______________________________

Review: Contractions

Draw lines from the words in the left column to the contractions in the right column.

cannot

did not

I am

we are

I have

is not

do not

I will

you are

it is

they will

I've

didn't

can't

we're

isn't

you're

it's

they'll

don't

I'm

I'll

Read Gabby's paragraph about four animals she saw at the zoo. Draw a line through each incorrect word. Write the correct word above it. There are three mistakes.

isn't
Example: That book ~~aren~~'t about snakes.

Seals and sea lions can swim but they isn't fish. A bat can fly but it isnt a bird. An armadillo is covered with bony plates but it aren't a reptile. Seals, sea lions, bats, and armadillos are all mammals.

Write two sentences about animals that are different. Use **isn't** and **aren't**.

Example: Zebras and giraffes aren't the same.
A zebra isn't as tall as a giraffe.

1. ______________________________

2. ______________________________

Wasn't, Weren't

Wasn't and weren't are two more contractions.

Use wasn't when you talk about one.

Gabby wasn't at the clubhouse.

Use weren't when you talk about more than one and with the word you.

Tiger and Gator weren't at the clubhouse, either.
You weren't able to find them right away.

Read this paragraph that Little Critter's mom wrote about him. She left out the words **wasn't** and **weren't**. Write the correct word in each blank.

You were looking for your friends. They ______________ playing ball. Tiger ______________ at the karate school. Gabby ______________ at the library. Gator ______________ in his backyard. ______________ you surprised to find them at your house, looking for you?

Bun Bun's thank you note has three mistakes. Draw a line through each incorrect word. Write the correct word above it.

weren't
Example: You ~~wasn't~~ late.

Dear Mrs. Critter,

Thank you for taking me to the circus. Weren't it fun? I weren't really scared. I knew those two acrobats weren't going to fall. You wasn't scared, were you?

Love,

Bun Bun

Write two sentences. Use **wasn't** or **weren't** in each sentence.

Example: The car wasn't big.
The clowns weren't happy.

1. ______________________________

2. ______________________________

Review: Contractions

Draw lines from the words in the left column to the contractions in the right column.

cannot	I've
did not	didn't
I am	can't
we are	we're
I have	isn't
is not	you're
do not	it's
I will	they'll
you are	don't
it is	I'm
they will	I'll

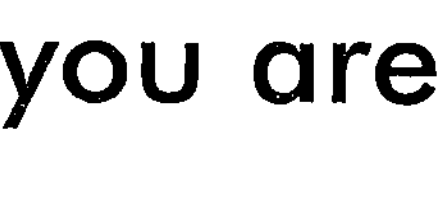

Fill in the blanks with the verb that shows that the action happened in the past.

1. Little Critter ____________ the ball to Tiger.
   kick, kicked

2. Little Sister ____________ to play, too.
   want, wanted

3. Little Critter and Tiger ____________ to her.
   call, called

4. Little Sister ____________ over.
   rush, rushed

5. They all ____________ ball.
   play, played

Write two sentences about something you did last week. Use action words with **-ed** on the end.

Example: Little Sister and I played in the rain.

1. ____

____

2. ____

____

Review: Adding -ed, -s

Fill in each blank. Show that the action happened in the past.

1. Last week, Malcolm ______________ his old toy drum.
   play

2. He ______________ on it with a wooden spoon.
   bang

3. The neighbors ______________ their ears.
   cover

4. Malcolm's grandma ______________ the window.
   close

Fill in each blank. Show that the action happened in the past.

1. Little Critter ______________ for his homework.
   hunt

2. He ______________ around in his closet.
   poke

3. He ______________ under the couch.
   reach

4. Then he ______________ his dog Blue.
   chase

Choose the correct form of the verb. Write your answer in each blank. Read each sentence aloud to see if it sounds right.

1. Gabby ______________ next door to Little Critter.
live, lives

2. Gator ______________ his room.
clean, cleaned

3. Bat Child ______________ jokes and ______________ to do magic tricks.
tell, tells — love, loves

4. Miss Kitty ______________ at Critterville Elementary.
work, works

These are Little Sister's directions for making breakfast. Look at the underlined words. If the wrong verb is used, cross it out. Write the correct verb above it. There are five mistakes. Read the sentences aloud to help you find the mistakes.

First you <u>opens</u> the box. Then you <u>pours</u> out the cereal. Oops, I forgot. You <u>need</u> a bowl. My big brother <u>add</u> milk for me. Sometimes, I <u>spills</u> the milk when I pour it. Then I <u>eats</u> my breakfast.

Using I

When you talk about what you do or who you are, use the word I.

Always write I with a capital letter. I is a pronoun that is used as a subject.

I helped my mom today.

When you talk about yourself and someone else, speak of yourself last.

Yes: Mom and I planted flowers.
No: I and Mom planted flowers.

Help Little Critter finish this story. Write I in the blanks. Then read each sentence to a friend.

Mom asked me to show her how a robot acts. ________ marched across the room. Then she asked me to work hard like a robot. ________ put my toys away. ________ also gave Mom my dirty shirts and socks. ________ think Mom tricked me into cleaning my room!

Little Critter's journal entry has three mistakes. Cross out each mistake. Write the correct word or words above it.

I

Example: Mom and ~~me~~ ate breakfast.

I and Dad were busy today. We worked outside. i pulled weeds and planted flowers. Gabby came over. Dad, Gabby, and I watered the new plants. Gabby and i got dirty. I had lots of fun.

Write two sentences to tell about something you and someone else did.

1. ______________________________

2. ______________________________

Handwriting Check

Look at your handwriting above. Are your words sitting on the line? Did you take your time and use your best handwriting? Did you put spaces between your words? Do your tall letters touch the top line and your small letters fit between the dotted and the lower lines?

How did you do?
(circle one)

Great!

Good!

O.K.

I'll do better next time.

Using Me

Sometimes when you talk about yourself, you are not the main person the sentence is about. In this case, use the word me.
Me is a pronoun, just like **I** is.

Mom walked with me to the pool.

When you talk about yourself and someone else, speak of yourself last.

Little Critter came with Mom and me.

Fill in each blank with the correct word or words.

1. My brother chased ________ through the house.
   I, me

2. He wanted ________ to leave him alone.
   I, me

3. Mom told ________________________________
   me and Little Critter, Little Critter and me

   to stop running through the house.

4. So I ran outside, and Little Critter kept chasing ________!
   I, me

Find the four mistakes in this story. Draw a line through the incorrect word or words. Write the correct word or words above them.

Bun Bun and me
Example: They were waiting for ~~me and Bun Bun~~.

Dad and I have a secret. It is just between Dad and I. Dad told it to I last night. He said he knew I would not tell. He said it was only for me and him. Mom wants me and Dad to tell her the secret. We can't! The secret is about Mom's birthday present.

Write two sentences about times when someone did something for you. Be sure to use **me** in each one.

1. ______________________________

2. ______________________________

Review: I, Me

Read this paragraph. Write **I** or **me** in each blank.

Gabby and ________ went to Snow Hill. She and ________ wanted to go sledding. Gabby went first. Then she gave the sled to ________ . She waited for me at the bottom of the hill. Next, she and ________ rode on the sled together. The sled went very fast with both Gabby and ________ on it.

Find the three mistakes in this story. Draw a line through the incorrect word. Write the correct word above it.

Example: He called ~~I~~ me on the phone.

Me like to sleep with my teddy bear. He makes me feel safe at night. The dark does not bother I when Teddy is watching. I don't tell my friends about my teddy. I think they might laugh. Dad told I he used to sleep with a teddy bear.

Read each sentence. Choose the correct answer and write it in the blank.

1. Both ____________________ wanted to go to the library.
Dad and me, Dad and I

2. ________ needed a book for a book report.
I, me

3. Little Sister wanted to come with ____________________.
Dad and me, Dad and I

4. ____________________ went to the children's section.
Little Sister and I, Little Sister and me

5. I found the book ________ needed.
I, me

6. Dad helped ________ check it out.
I, me

7. ________ ran to the car with my book.
I, me

8. Little Sister ran behind ________ .
I, me

Rhyming Words

Rhyming words are very helpful when you want to write poetry and songs, or when you want to add interest to stories you write.

Read the poem. Circle the rhyming words.

Mr. Rubble is a man

Who collects a lot of things

Like buoy bells, an old tin can,

A smelly sock, and mattress springs.

Do you need a broken clock?

Rusty rings? Some oyster shells?

A frying pan? A cinder block?

Mr. Rubble buys and sells.

Challenge: Look for other poems in this workbook. Find all of the rhyming words that you can.

The rhyming words from the poem on page 106 are listed below. Add your own rhyming words to each list.

sock/clock/block

____

____

____

____

pan/can/man

____

____

____

____

things/springs/rings

____

____

____

____

bells/shells/sells

____

____

____

____

Bat Child wants to tell you about himself in some rhymes he wrote. Help him finish each rhyme by filling in the blank with a word that rhymes with the word in red.

My name is Bat Child. I'm a funny guy,
My favorite dessert is mosquito __________.

I have a little sister named Baby Bat,
She likes to torment our dear, old __________.

I'm a magician if you didn't know,
So have a seat and enjoy the __________.

Abracadabra-Kalamaroo,
Let's disappear and go to the __________.

Compound Words

A compound word is a **big** word made up of **two** smaller words. Write the compound word for each picture below

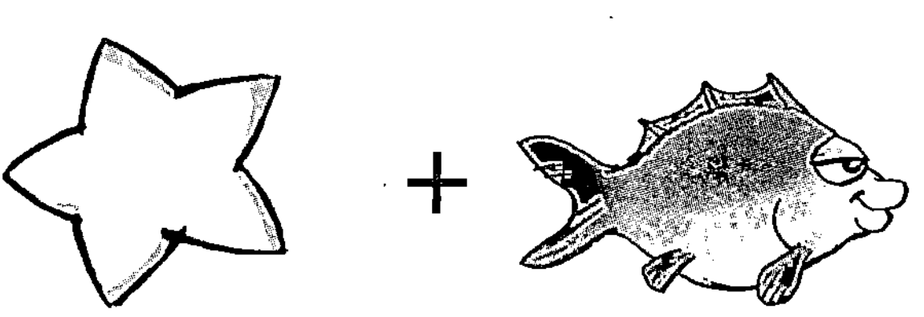

starfish

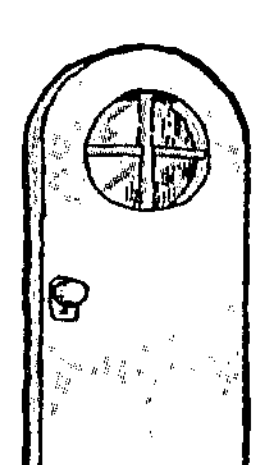 + 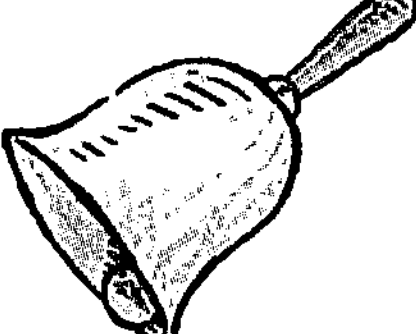

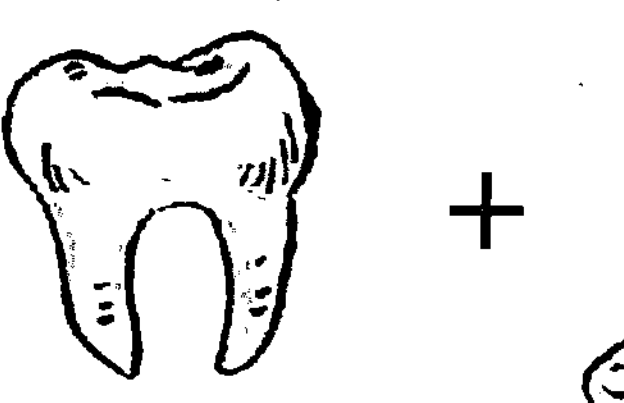 + 

 + 

 + 

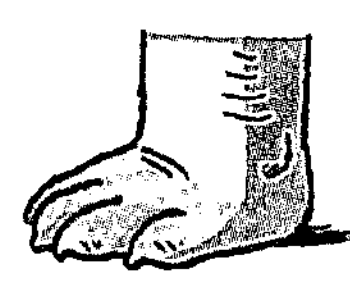 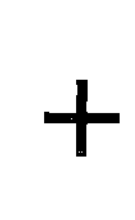 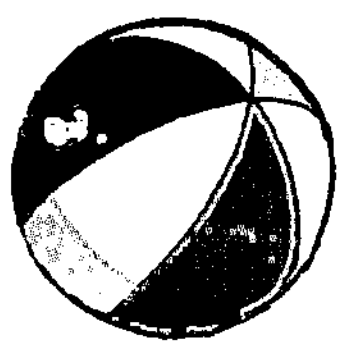

 + 

 + 

Tiger got his compound words a little mixed up. Circle the incorrect words. Rewrite each sentence with the correct compound word from the box below.

snowball	driveway	football	sunburn

1. We had a snowflake fight last winter.

2. I got a sunrise at the beach.

3. We played basketball on the runway.

4. I threw the footprints as hard as I could down the field.

Challenge: Make a list of all the compound words you can think of. Ask friends and family to help you. Keep your list below.

Common Nouns

Nouns are parts of speech. A common noun names any person, place, or thing.

Person	Place	Thing
teacher	school	pencil
baby	park	bottle

Make a list of all the common nouns you can find in the picture. Put them in the correct column.

Person	Place	Thing
police officer	sewer	stairs
boy	street	book

Read the paragraph below. Write a common noun in each blank.

I really wanted a new __________. I asked my __________ whether I could have one. I had to earn money. I made __________ and sold them. I cleaned the __________. Finally I went to the __________ and bought a __________ with the money I earned.

Write a sentence about a pet. Underline the common nouns.

Reread your sentence. Change some of the common nouns to make the sentence funny. Rewrite the sentence.

Using **a** and **an**

The words a and an help point out a noun. Use a before consonant sounds. Use an before vowel sounds.

a	b	c	d	e	f	g	h	i	j	k	l	m
n	o	p	q	r	s	t	u	v	w	x	y	z

Examples:

an **apple**	a **banana**
an **egg**	a **chicken**
an **insect**	a **fish**
an **octopus**	a **raindrop**
an **umbrella**	a **snowflake**

Little Critter is packing for a trip! Look in his suitcase to see what he packed. Make a list of all the things he packed. Use **a** or **an** in your list. Circle the thing he probably shouldn't have packed.

____

____

______________________________ ______________________________

______________________________ ______________________________

______________________________ ______________________________

______________________________ ______________________________

Fill in the blanks with **a** or **an**.

Mom sent Little Critter to Molini's Market to buy ______ loaf of bread, ______ onion, and ______ quart of milk. When he got there he forgot what mom wanted. He bought ______ apple, ______ box of cookies, and ______ quart of orange juice. When he got home, he showed Mom the groceries. She sent Little Critter back to the store. This time she gave him ______ list.

Look at all the things around you. Make a list of things you see. Place them in the appropriate column.

a	an

Common and Proper Nouns

A common noun names any person, place, or thing.

A proper noun names a special person, a special place, or a special thing. A proper noun begins with a capital letter.

Mr. Molini **lives in the** town **of** Critterville**.**

Place each word in the word bank in the correct column. Fill the blanks with words of your own.

Word Bank			
Critterville	ball	Texas	library
boat	Little Sister	road	Main Street
Canada	town	country	Hogley's Hardware
Molini's Market	boy	Gabby	mountain

proper nouns	common nouns
Critterville	ball
______	______
______	______
______	______
______	______
______	______
______	______
______	______
______	______

Read the paragraph below. Write a proper noun in each blank.

My name is ___________. I am on a secret mission to find out why all the students at ___________ School in ___________ make animal sounds. First, I asked ___________, and he barked. Then I asked ___________, and she meowed. The mystery was solved. They all wanted to be the teacher's pet!

Write one sentence that tells about a special person or place. Circle the proper noun.

Think of one more proper noun to add to your sentence. Rewrite the sentence.

Pronouns

Pronouns take the place of nouns. These replacements must be chosen very carefully. Some pronouns you might use are: I, me, you, he, she, him, it, we, us, they, them, my, mine, your, his, her, hers, its, ours, and their.

Examples:

Bat Child tells jokes. → He tells jokes.

Maurice and Molly are twins. → They are twins.

The car broke down. → It broke down.

Little Sister danced in a recital. → She danced in a recital.

__________ worked hard. → I worked hard.
your name

Read Bat Child's riddles below. Circle every pronoun.

What should I say if I meet a monster with three heads?

"Hello. How are you? Hello. How are you? Hello. How are you?"

Why did the bat want to become a photographer?

She loved being in dark rooms.

Why did it take a bookworm ten months to finish a book?

He wasn't very hungry.

Read the paragraph below. Write a pronoun in each blank.

Maurice and Molly went to the store with their mother. _______ were getting a birthday gift for Little Critter. "I wonder what _______ would like?" asked _______ mother. "_______ think he would like a football," said Molly. "I think _______ would like some new paints and paper," said Maurice. Their mom said "Here is a Super Critter doll. _______ has a red cape and _______ talks when you pull this string. What do _______ think?" she asked. "That's cool! Let's get ____!" said Maurice and Molly.

Write a sentence about a funny toy or a funny birthday present.

Replace the noun you used above with a pronoun and rewrite your sentence.

Verbs

Verbs are parts of speech that can show action. They tell what is happening. Without action verbs, nothing would get done!

Little Sister walked to the edge of the pool. She dipped her toe in to see if the water was cold. She held her nose and got ready to jump.

"Go on and jump," Dad told Little Sister. "I'll catch you!"

Read Little Sister's poem about the Critter's family vacation. Circle eight action verbs.

We went on vacation.

We saw lots of things.

We slept in a motel.

I played on the swings.

I pulled on my swimsuit.

I walked to the pool.

I jumped in the water.

I think I'm so cool.

Read the paragraph below about Little Critter's trip to an amusement park. Write an action verb in each blank.

My family and I _______ Critterland. We _______ around and around on our first ride. We _______ over and over on the next ride. When we got on the roller coaster, we _______ up and down.

Write a sentence that tells what might happen at the amusement park next. Underline your action verb.

Reread your sentence. Substitute a new action verb for the original verb. Rewrite the sentence. Underline the new action verb.

Action and Linking Verbs

Action verbs show action.

Little Critter washes the dishes.

Linking verbs help tell about the subject.

Little Critter is thoughtful.

Here are some examples of linking verbs:

am was is were are be

In the sentences below, circle the action verbs and draw a box around the linking verbs.

Little Critter peeled the carrots.

Little Sister washed the potatoes.

They were very helpful.

Mom cooked the vegetables.

Dad sliced the meat.

Everyone was hungry.

Blue waited under the table for scraps.

Little Critter handed Blue something to eat.

Dinner was delicious.

Blue thought so, too.

Make a list of **action verbs.** Try to think of at least three different words.

Make a list of **linking verbs.**

Pick three of your action verbs. Use them in sentences below.

1.

2.

3.

Pick three of your linking verbs. Use them in sentences below.

1.

2.

3.

Review: Nouns, Pronouns, Verbs

Read the paragraph. Write a common noun in each blank.

Mom said that it was time to clean my _______. I had not done this for two _______, so it was a little messy. First, I looked under my _______. I was surprised to find my _______! When I looked in the _______, I saw my _______! When I opened the _______, my _______ fell out!

Read the story below. Circle the seven proper nouns.

Maurice and Molly did not know what to do. Their favorite movie theater, Super Cinema, was closed. They went to the Play Until Dark Park, but it was closed. Finally, Maurice and Molly rode their bikes to the Critterville Library. The bike rack was full. Everyone else was looking for something to do, too.

Read the story below. Draw a line under each pronoun. Look back on page 116 if you need help remembering pronouns.

The knight was upset. He did not know what to do. The king and queen had asked him to find a dragon. They wanted to put it in the Royal Zoo. The poor knight sat down on a rock. He knew that no dragons existed. They had not lived for many years.

The knight sat for hours. No ideas came to him. Then a dragonfly landed next to him. He picked it up and brought it to the king and queen. They were happy. They had their dragon at last!

Read the sentences. Draw a circle around each verb.

1. Mom, Little Sister, and Little Critter made cookies.
2. Little Sister rolled out the dough.
3. Little Critter cut out the shapes with cookie cutters.
4. Then mom put them in the oven.
5. The cookies cooled on the counter.
6. Finally, everyone decorated the cookies and ate them.
7. They were delicious.

Adjectives

Adjectives describe nouns and pronouns. They are parts of speech that help paint a picture in your mind.

Little Critter's striped pajamas are black and white. Little Sister's spotted pajamas are orange and brown. Little Critter and Little Sister look like they belong at the zoo.

Read the story below. Circle the adjectives.

Miss Kitty is a good teacher. She took her class on a fascinating field trip to the zoo. It was a beautiful day. The sun was high in the bright blue sky. The students saw huge elephants, graceful giraffes, and peaceful zebras. They ate a delicious picnic lunch under an old oak tree and sang silly songs on the long bus ride home. Everybody had a great time and learned a lot.

After the field trip, Miss Kitty had her students write about their day. Help the children add some adjectives to their writing to make it more interesting. Write an adjective in each space. Draw a picture to match each sentence.

The ________________ bus took us to the zoo. It was a ________________ ride.

We saw a ________________ bird sitting in a ________________ tree.

A ________________ snake slithered through the ________________ grass.

Some ____________ zebras were eating ________________ grass for their dinner.

It was a ____________ day. Miss Kitty is a ________________ teacher.

Practice Page

Use this page for extra practice.

First Word in a Sentence

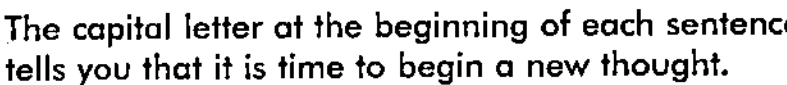

Use a capital letter to begin each sentence. The capital is like a sign that says "START HERE."

The capital letter at the beginning of each sentence tells you that it is time to begin a new thought.

Little Critter wrote a story. Help him proofread the first paragraph. Write this mark ≡ to show the letters that should be capitalized. Write the capital letters above.

M H
mouse is a great pet. he likes to run all around my room.

S H
sometimes I let him ride in my pocket. he lives in a cage on

M
my bookshelf. mouse enjoys running on his exercise wheel.

H
he likes to shred up paper to make

M
a soft bed. mouse is my friend.

Read Gabby's story about an unhappy bird. Use this mark ≡ to show the four letters that should be capitalized. Write a capital letter above each one.

T
Example: they are going to the store to buy some milk.

F T
The little bird was lost. first, he flew to a pine tree. then

F
he flew to an oak tree. finally, he heard his mother's chirp.

T
then he knew just where to fly.

Write two sentences about the picture. Begin each sentence with a capital letter.

1. Sentences will vary.

2.

The Word I

The word **I** is always a capital letter.

You are a very important person. When you use **I** in place of your name, make it a capital letter.

I love sports!

My friends and I play soccer.

Playing soccer is something I like to do.

Tiger wrote a poem. Use this mark ≡ to show each letter that should be a capital letter. Write the capital letter above each one.

I
My friend and i went hiking.

We walked down River Road.

I
i found a caterpillar,

I
and then i caught a toad.

My friend dug up some worms.

I
i helped him dig the hole.

We could be catching lots of fish,

I
if i just had a pole.

Read Little Critter's riddles below. Use this mark ≡ to show the six letters that should be capitalized. Write the capital letter above each one.

I I
- I am an insect and i can do what I am. What am i ?

I
i am a fly!

I I
- i am round on the ends and high in the middle. What am i ?

I
i am Ohio!

Pretend you are a football or soccer player. Write two sentences about what you would be doing. Use capital letters where they are needed.

1. Sentences will vary.

2.

Handwriting Check

Look at your handwriting above. Are your words sitting on the line? Did you take your time and use your best handwriting? Did you put spaces between your words? Do your tall letters touch the top line and your small letters fit between the dotted and the lower lines?

How did you do? (circle one)

Great!

Good!

O.K.

I'll do better next time.

People and Pets

A person's (or a critter's) name, or a pet's name always begins with a capital letter.

Little Critter took his dog Blue for a walk in the park. He saw Molly and Maurice on the swings.

Draw a picture of someone you know with his or her pet. Write your friend's name and the animal's name under the picture.

Pictures will vary.

Write a sentence about your picture. Use names in your sentence.

Sentences will vary.

Little Critter has lots of pets. Pretend you are Little Critter, and give all of your pets different names. Begin each name with a capital letter.

Answers will vary.

Write the names of six people you know. Use a capital letter for the first letter of every name.

1. Answers will vary.
2.
3.
4.
5.
6.

Titles of Respect

Miss, Mrs., Ms., and Mr. are titles of respect and should be used before certain names. Begin each title with a capital letter.

Use the proofreader's mark to show the letters that should be capitalized. Write the capital letter above.

Miss Kitty

M
ms. Dingo

M
mr. Hogley

M
mrs. Critter

Draw a picture of an adult you know. Write that person's name on the line.

Answers will vary.

Welcome to Critterville! Meet some more critters who live and work in Critterville. Use the word bank to label the critters with their correct names. Make sure their names and titles of respect start with capital letters.

Write two sentences about the folks in Critterville. Here is an example:

Mrs. Molini works at Molini's Market.

1. Sentences will vary.

2.

Review: Capitalization

Rewrite each red sentence correctly using the tips to help you.

Use a capital letter to begin a sentence.

this sentence starts with a capital letter.

This sentence starts with a capital letter.

The word **I** is always a capital letter.

i always try to do my best work.

I always try to do my best work.

A person's name or a pet's name always begins with a capital letter.

little critter has a dog named blue.

Little Critter has a dog named Blue.

Miss, Mrs., Ms., and Mr. should begin with a capital letter.

miss Kitty is a great teacher.

Miss Kitty is a great teacher.

Read Gabby's sentences below. Use this mark ≡ to show the letters that should be capitalized. Write the capital letter above each one.

M M
1. maurice and molly love to read books.

M M C M K
2. mr. and mrs. critter help out in miss kitty's class.

Read the paragraph below. Write this mark ≡ under the letters that should be capitalized. Write the capital letter above each one.

L S I
little sister and i have a lot of fun together. (W) we go to the park almost every day in the summer. (I) i like to look for frogs. (L S) little sister likes to climb on the monkey bars. (W G) when grandma and (G) grandpa come to visit, they go to the park with us. (W) we usually pack a picnic lunch to take along. Sometimes we see (M) ms. (G) greene, the park ranger. (S) she does a great job taking care of the park. (I) i once gave her a cookie to thank her.

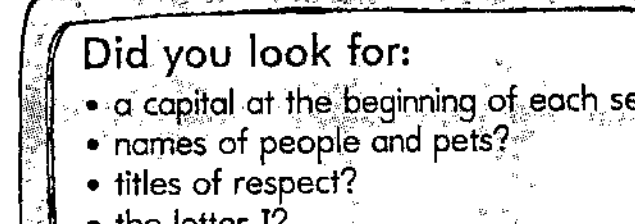

Places

There are many kinds of places. Use a capital letter for the first letter of the name of each special place.

Tiger visited the Critterville Zoo. (zoo)

Gator is from North Carolina. (state)

Gabby stayed overnight in Orlando. (city)

Bun Bun lives on Sweet Street. (street)

Little Critter goes to Critterville School. (school)

Malcolm was born in the United States of America. (country)

Learn about Critterville. Use this mark ≡ to show the letters that should be capitalized. Write the capital letter above each one. See if you can find all nine words that need to be corrected.

A
Ms. Dingo is from australia.

T S
The junkyard is on treasure street.

Ms. Dingo

C Z
The critterville zoo is a fun place to visit.

N Y C
Mr. Stork used to live in new york city.

Mr. Stork

M
Miss Kitty was born in michigan.

Miss Kitty

Fill in the blanks below. Don't forget to use capital letters.

I live in Answers will vary.
(name of country)

I live in ______________________.
(name of state)

I live in ______________________.
(name of city)

I live on ______________________.
(name of street)

I go to ______________________.
(name of school)

Read Gabby's book report. Use this mark ≡ to show the words that should be capitalized. Write the capital letter above each one.

I read a mystery that took place in the (U) united (S) states of (A) america. The detective finds the first clue on (M) mt. (W) wilson in (C) california. She finds the second clue beside (L) lake (O) okeechobee in (F) florida. She solves the mystery on (E) elm (S) street in her own backyard.

Days and Months

There are seven days in a week and 12 months in a year. These words always begin with a capital letter.

Days
Sunday
Monday
Tuesday
Wednesday
Thursday
Friday
Saturday

Months	
January	July
February	August
March	September
April	October
May	November
June	December

The names of the months are all scrambled. Unscramble the letters and rewrite the months using a capital letter at the beginning of each month.

1. ujyarna January
2. yulj July
3. teroocb October
4. guatus August
5. lapir April
6. ryerbuaf February
7. amy May
8. rbonmeve November
9. embespter September
10. enju June
11. mbdceere December
12. arcmh March

Circle your favorite month. Write a sentence about why it is your favorite.

Sentences will vary.

Look at Little Critter's calendar. Fill in the missing days of the week.

August						
Sunday	Monday	Tuesday	Wednesday	Thursday	Friday	Saturday
			1	2	3	4 Birthday party
5	6	7 Last soccer game	8	9	10	11
12	13	14	15 Dentist 10:00	16	17	18
19	20	21	22	23	24 Pool closes	25
26	27 First day of school	28	29	30	31	

Now use the calendar to fill in the blanks with the correct day of the week.
Example: The first day of school is on a Monday.

1. The Critterville Pool closes for the summer on a Friday
2. Little Critter is going to a party on a Saturday
3. Little Critter is going to the dentist on a Wednesday
4. The last soccer game is on a Tuesday

Friendly Letters

1) Date: Begin with a date at the top. Always use a capital letter for the name of the month.

2) Greeting: Start your greeting with Dear. Then write your friend's name. Begin each word with a capital letter.

3) Body: The body of a letter is what you want to tell your friend. Use capital letters to begin each sentence.

4) Closing: End the letter with a closing and your name. Use a capital letter to begin the closing. Your name should start with a capital letter, too.

August 31, 2001

Dear Friend,

My name is Little Critter. I have a younger sister. She is two years younger than I am. My friends' names are Gator, Gabby, Bun Bun, Tiger, Maurice, and Molly. I live with my mom and dad. My teacher's name is Miss Kitty. She makes school a lot of fun. I like to play baseball and ride my bike. This summer I went camping with my dad. Please write back and tell me about yourself.

Sincerely,
Little Critter

Now it is your turn. Write a letter back to Little Critter. Tell him at least three things about yourself. Don't forget to use capital letters.

Date

Greeting

Answers will vary.

Closing

(your name)

Editing Checklist:
I used capital letters for the:
- ☐ date
- ☐ greeting
- ☐ beginning of a sentence
- ☐ closing
- ☐ names
- ☐ the word I

Review: Capitalization

Rewrite each red sentence correctly using the tips to help you.

- Use a capital letter for the days of the week and the months of the year.

july 4th is Independence Day.

July 4th is Independence Day.

- Use a capital letter for the names of cities or towns.

critterville is a great place to live.

Critterville is a great place to live.

- Use a capital letter in the dates, greetings, and closings of friendly letters.

july 5, 2002

dear grandma,

Thanks for taking me to the fireworks. It was fun.

love,

little critter

July 5, 2002

Dear Grandma,

Thanks for taking me to the fireworks. It was fun.

Love,

Little Critter

Gator wrote a letter at camp. Use this mark ≡ to show where he needs capital letters. Write the capital letter above each mark.

J
july 31, 2001

D
dear Little Critter,

T T C A
today is tuesday. camp Critter is really neat. all the

I F H
bugs are very big. i have a spider named fuzzy. her legs

I M S
have a lot of hair. i put her in a jar on monday. spike is my

H K
snake. he sleeps with me in my sleeping bag. kyle, our

S I
camp leader, doesn't know about spike. i will show you

S F A I
spike and fuzzy when I come home in august. i cannot wait

to see what I will find tomorrow!

S
sincerely,

G
gator

Did you look for a capital at the beginning of:
- each sentence?
- names of special places?
- the word I?
- names of people and pets?
- the date, greeting, and closing?
- days of the week and months of the year?

Complete Thoughts

A sentence tells a complete thought.

This is a sentence, because it is a complete thought.

Little Critter is excited about his birthday.

This is not a sentence, because it does not tell a complete thought.

A birthday cake.

Circle each group of words that forms a complete thought.

- (Little Critter went into the house.)
- (It was quiet.)
- Into the living room.
- (He turned on the light.)
- A surprise.
- (Everyone popped out from behind the furniture.)
- Laughing hard.

Subjects and Verbs

Every sentence has two parts, the naming part and the telling part. The naming part of a sentence tells who or what the sentence is about. The naming part is also called the subject of the sentence.

Tiger hid behind the couch.
The room was dark.

To Do: Look at your circled sentences on page 24. Underline the naming part or subject of each sentence.

The telling part of a sentence tells what someone or something is or does. The telling part of a sentence is also called the verb.

Tiger hid behind the couch.
The room was dark.

To Do: Look at your circled sentences on page 24 again. Use two lines to underline the verbs in your circled sentences.

Write a verb for each sentence. Then circle the subject(s) or naming part(s) in each sentence.

Sample answers given.

(Gator and Tiger) yelled, "Surprise!"

(Everyone) sang "Happy Birthday."

(Little Critter) had a great birthday.

Periods

A period is like a stop sign. It tells the reader that a sentence has ended.

Little Critter likes to eat at Critterville Diner.

He always orders spaghetti with meatballs.

Put this mark ⊙ at the end of each sentence.

Little Sister likes apple pie with ice cream⊙ Dad loves cheese and crackers⊙ Bun Bun has carrots for a snack when she gets home from school⊙ Grandma Critter likes to make vegetable soup⊙ Mom and Little Critter enjoy juicy watermelon on hot summer days⊙ Miss Kitty always has a cookie and a glass of milk when the school day is done⊙

Proofreader's Toolbox
Use this mark ⊙ at the end of a sentence to show where a period is needed.

Read the story below. Five periods are missing. Use this mark ⊙ to add periods where they belong.

Little Critter was hungry⊙ He decided to make his favorite sandwich. First, he got two slices of bread⊙ Then, he spread some peanut butter on them. Next, he put on some pickles⊙ Finally, he added potato chips and orange juice. Little Criter took a bite⊙ His sandwich was delicious⊙

Write two sentences that tell something about a food you like. End each sentence with a period.

1. Sentences will vary.

2.

A sentence tells a complete thought. There are four different kinds of sentences. They are: statements, questions, exclamations, and commands.

Statements

A statement is a sentence that tells about something. Its first word begins with a capital letter. Use a period to end a sentence that tells about something.

Maurice is holding his picture.

Molly is reading a story.

Here are some statements about Maurice and Molly. Use these marks ≡ and ⊙ to show that the statements start with a capital letter and end with a period.

M
maurice and Molly are twins⊙

M
molly is two minutes and twenty seconds older than maurice⊙

M
molly likes to write about butterflies⊙

M
maurice likes to draw pictures of dolphins⊙

Maurice and Molly wrote some statements. Rewrite them using capital letters and periods correctly. Try to decide who wrote each statement. Check the box to show your guess.

	Maurice	Molly
dolphins play games in the water	☑	☐
Dolphins play games in the water.		
a butterfly is a grown-up caterpillar	☐	☑
A butterfly is a grown-up caterpillar.		
it is fun to have a brother	☐	☑
It is fun to have a brother.		
i am older	☐	☑
I am older.		
my twin sister wrote a story	☑	☐
My twin sister wrote a story.		

Write two statements about yourself.

1. Sentences will vary.

2.

Questions

All questions need me.
What am I?
I am a question mark.

A question is a sentence that asks something. Its first word begins with a capital letter. The sentence ends with a question mark.

What will I be when I grow up?

Taller.

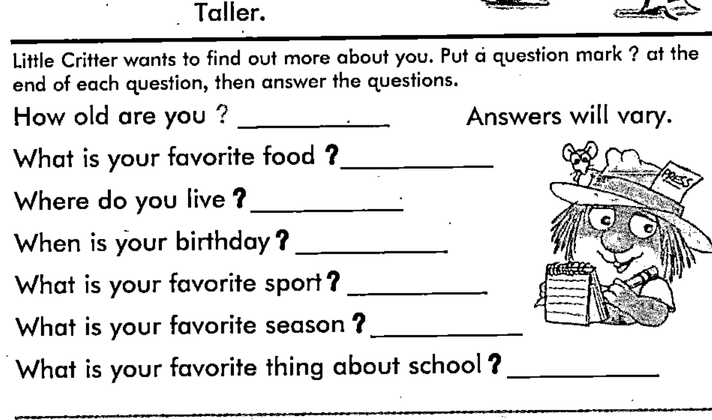

Little Critter wants to find out more about you. Put a question mark ? at the end of each question, then answer the questions.

How old are you ? ________ Answers will vary.

What is your favorite food **?**________

Where do you live **?**________

When is your birthday **?**________

What is your favorite sport **?**________

What is your favorite season **?**________

What is your favorite thing about school **?**________

You can write a letter to Little Critter on his Web site. Tell him all about yourself. His Web address is:

http://www.littlecritter.com/write_letter.html

Bat Child forgot to use question marks. Put them in the places where they belong.

Knock, knock.
Who's there**?**
Owl.
Owl who **?**
Owl you know unless you open the door**?**

Knock, knock.
Who's there**?**
Max.
Max who **?**
Max no difference. Just open the door.

Knock, knock.
Who's there**?**
Police.
Police who**?**
Police let me in. It's cold out here.

Challenge: Look for question marks in books you read. Make a list of words that you often find at the beginning of questions.

Exclamations

An exclamation is a sentence that shows surprise or excitement. Its first word begins with a capital letter. The sentence ends with an exclamation point.

Oh, no!

A shark!

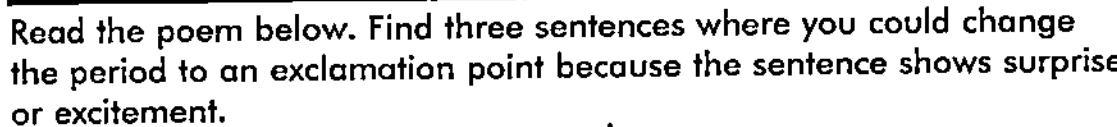

Read the poem below. Find three sentences where you could change the period to an exclamation point because the sentence shows surprise or excitement.

I swam around. The sea was calm.
My boat was right nearby.
And then I saw a fin I knew.
A shark was close**!** Oh, my**!**

I saw his teeth, his rows of teeth.
His jaws were quite a sight.
And he was coming straight for me.
I was his next big bite**!**

I swam so fast, I reached my boat.
I landed dripping wet.
And then my mom called from the hall,
"Are you done with your bath yet?"

Uh, oh! Little Critter used too many exclamation points. Read the poem and decide where he should have used a period instead. Cross out each unnecessary exclamation point and put this mark ⊙ in its place.

My dad and I went hiking!⊙
We hiked from here to there!⊙
We tramped along the trail!⊙
And then we saw a bear!

The bear was picking berries!⊙
I liked that furry beast!⊙
But since the bear was going west,
My dad and I went east!

Now reread the poem. Practice reading exclamation points. Add excitement to your voice when you come to an exclamation point at the end of a sentence.

Write two exciting sentences about swimming. Be sure to end each with an exclamation point.

1. Sentences will vary.

2. ________

Exclamation points are like periods that explode with excitement! Be careful not to use them too much. Save them for something really exciting.

Commands

A command is a sentence that gives directions or orders. Its first word begins with a capital letter. The sentence ends with a period or an exclamation point.

The Coach said, "Run five warm up laps. Then do twenty jumping jacks. Okay, go!"

Read the conversations below. Underline all of the commands.

Dad was giving Little Critter tips on how to play checkers. "Think two or three moves ahead. Set up your jumps. Be a good sport."

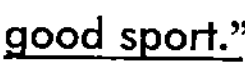

Little Critter's class went apple picking. Miss Kitty taught her students how to make applesauce. "First get permission and help from your parents. Wash your hands. Then peel and cut up your apples. Put the apples in a pan. Add sugar and cinnamon. Let them cook until they are soft. Mash up the cooked apples. Let the mixture cool before you eat it."

Write three command sentences that a coach, a teacher, or a parent might say.

1. Sentences will vary.

2.

3.

Handwriting Check

Look at your handwriting above. Are your words sitting on the line? Did you take your time and use your best handwriting? Did you put spaces between your words? Do your tall letters touch the top line and your small letters fit between the dotted and the lower lines?

How did you do? (circle one)

Great!

Good!

O.K.

I'll do better next time.

Review: Sentences and Punctuation

Read the story below carefully. Underline the three statements. Draw a circle around the question. Draw two lines under the two exclamations. Draw a box around the command. Add the proper marks at the end of each sentence.

The snow fell all night. Today is a snow day! Let's go sledding down Critterville Hill. I will bring my sled. Can you bring your inner tube? Great! We will have lots of fun.

Read the poem below. Put a period after six statements. Put a question mark after one question. Put an exclamation point after one exciting statement.

I was building a snowman in my yard.
Finding the snow was not too hard.
A big, big snowstorm came last night.
Everything here was covered in white.

The snowball I made started to roll.
It picked up speed and went out of control!
It got bigger and bigger on its way down.
Where would it stop when it rolled into town?

Read each sentence below. Decide whether it is a question, an exclamation, a command, or a statement. Circle the correct answer.

Little Critter, please take your sister sledding.
Statement Question Exclamation (Command)

I think this is the steepest hill in Critterville.
(Statement) Question Exclamation Command

Look how fast Tiger is going!
Statement Question (Exclamation) Command

Did you see Gabby and Gator going down on an inner tube?
Statement (Question) Exclamation Command

I always wear a hat and mittens when it is cold.
(Statement) Question Exclamation Command

Let's go down the hill one more time.
Statement Question Exclamation (Command)

Do you want marshmallows in your hot chocolate?
Statement (Question) Exclamation Command

That was a lot of fun!
Statement Question (Exclamation) Command

Cities and States

A comma goes between the name of a city and a state.

Columbus, Ohio

New York, New York

Denver, Colorado

Help Little Critter label these cities and states. The city names are in blue and the state names are in red. Write the city and state on the line. Place a comma between the name of the city and the state. Remember to use a capital letter at the beginning of the name of a city or state.

Columbus, Ohio

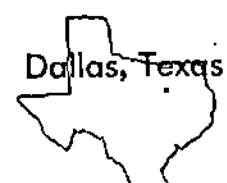

Dallas, Texas

Orlando, Florida

Juneau, Alaska

Fill in the blank with a city and state.

I live in

Answers will vary.

Someday I would like to visit

I know someone who lives in

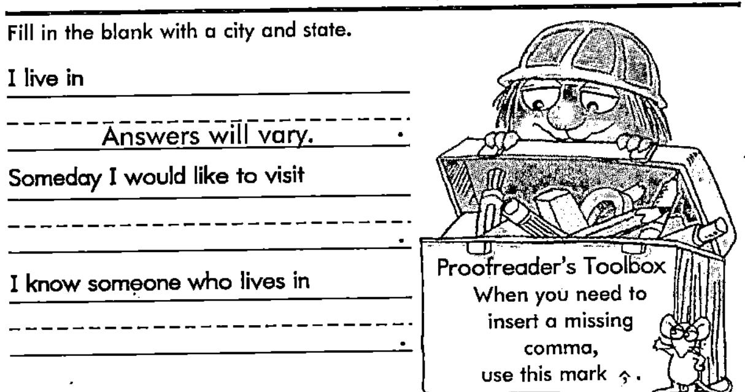

Proofreader's Toolbox
When you need to insert a missing comma, use this mark ^.

Add six commas where they are needed. Use this proofreader's mark ^.

Miss Kitty's class was studying funny names of cities in the United States. The students read about Boulder, Colorado. They wondered if the rocks in that city are bigger than the rocks in Little Rock, Arkansas. Do ghosts really live in Casper, Wyoming? Does everyone sew in Needles, California? The class decided that there must be a lot of bookstores in Reading, Pennsylvania. And they wondered if any aliens live in Neptune, Ohio.

Challenge: Use a map or an atlas to see if you can find more cities with funny names.

Commas in Friendly Letters

1) Date: Whenever you write a date, put a comma between the day and the year.

2) Greeting: Put a comma after the greeting.

3) Closing: A comma goes after the closing.

June 26, 2001

Dear Grandma,

I can't wait to go to the beach with you. Will you teach me how to surf?

Sincerely,
Little Critter

Add three commas to Grandma's letter. Use this proofreader's mark ^.

July 2, 2001

Dear Little Critter,

Since I don't know how to surf, I can't teach you, but I can show you how to build a sandcastle. I am looking forward to your visit. See you soon.

Sincerely,
Grandma

Pretend you are Little Critter. Write a letter to your mom and dad telling them all about your day at the beach with Grandma. Don't forget to use commas.

Date

Greeting

Answers will vary.

Closing

Little Critter

Commas in Lists

A comma goes between each person, place, thing, or phrase in a list.

Grandma has a wonderful garden. She grows beans, tomatoes, onions, and peppers.

Read each sentence below. Make the lists in the sentences easier to read by putting nine commas where they are needed. Use this proofreader's mark ^.

1. Little Critter has a dog, a cat, a fish, and a frog.
2. Miss Kitty called on Maurice, Molly, Gabby, and Gator during math class.
3. Little Critter likes peanut butter, pickles, potato chips, and orange juice on his sandwich.

Make a list of your three favorite foods and three favorite toys in the boxes below.

Foods:	Toys:
Answers will vary.	Answers will vary.

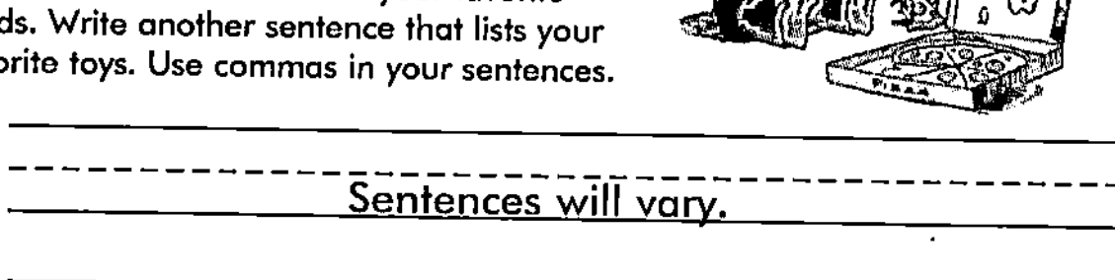

Write one sentence that lists your favorite foods. Write another sentence that lists your favorite toys. Use commas in your sentences.

1. Sentences will vary.
2.

Review: Commas

Read Gabby's story about Gabbilocks. Add five commas where they are needed.

Gabbilocks and the Three Bears

Gabbilocks was lost in the woods. She came to a house and went in. She thought that the three bowls of porridge were too hot, too cold, and just right. She thought that the three chairs were too hard, too soft, and just right. She found a bed and fell asleep. The bear family came home. Gabbilocks woke up and ran away. Then Gabbilocks visited her grandma in Honeyville, Maine. Grandma told her to write a letter to the bear family.

Add the commas in Gabbilocks' letter. Use this proofreader's mark ^.

June 10, 2001

Dear Bear Family,

I got lost in the woods. I went to your house because I was scared. I am sorry that I ate, sat, and slept in your house. Will you visit me in Honeyville, Maine? We have lots of fruit, nuts, and honey.

Sincerely,
Gabbilocks

Read the sentences below. Use this proofreader's mark ^ to add fourteen commas where they belong.

On August 10, 2001, Papa Bear, Mama Bear, and Baby Bear left the woods in a plane. They landed in Honeyville, Maine.

Gabbilocks met them at the airport. She was so pleased that they had come to visit her and her grandma.

At Grandma's house, they ate apples, oranges, berries, nuts, and pears. Gabbilocks gave Baby Bear a new chair. She made yellow, green, and blue cushions for Mama Bear and Papa Bear.

On August 12, 2001, the Bears had to return to Woods, Pennsylvania. The Bears thanked Gabbilocks and Grandma for all the food, fun, and presents. They also gave Gabbilocks a key to their house and invited her to come over whenever she wants.

Look back at your work.
Did you remember:
- ☐ commas in a list?
- ☐ commas in dates?
- ☐ commas in a city, state?

Quotation Marks in Dialogue

Quotation marks go before and after a speaker's words. Little Sister says, "Use quotation marks around words that someone says aloud."

Read Little Sister's silly sentences below. Circle each speaker's exact words.

1. (Does anybody have some glue?) asked Humpty Dumpty.
2. (We are so hungry, we could eat a house!) said Hansel and Gretel.
3. Prince Charming told Cinderella, (If the shoe fits, wear it.)
4. (Don't wolf down your food!) exclaimed Little Red Riding Hood.
5. The White Rabbit said, (Digital watches are best.)
6. The woman who swallowed a fly said, (Yuck!)

Finish the sentences below. Use the words from the cartoon. Remember to use quotation marks before and after a speaker's words.

Little Critter asked, "Will you teach me how to steal a base?"

Tiger replied, "Sure, but you have to promise to give it back."

Little Critter asked, " What's worse than finding a worm in an apple?"

Dad replied, "Finding half a worm."

Periods in Abbreviations

Some words can be made shorter or abbreviated. Abbreviations end with a period. Days of the week and months of the year can be abbreviated only when used in a date.

Examples:

Saturday, August 4, 2001 → Sat., Aug. 4, 2001
Monday, April 1, 2002 → Mon., Apr. 1, 2002

Days of the Week: Match the day of the week to the correct abbreviation.

Sunday	Thurs.
Monday	Sun.
Tuesday	Wed.
Wednesday	Mon.
Thursday	Fri.
Friday	Sat.
Saturday	Tues.

Months of the Year: Circle the abbreviations. Write the abbreviated word next to each month using a period. Hint: Use the first 3 letters of the month. For September, use the first four letters. May, June, and July are already short enough!

January	Jan.
February	Feb.
March	Mar.
April	Apr.
August	Aug.
September	Sept.
October	Oct.
November	Nov.
December	Dec.

Abbreviate the dates below. Don't forget to use a period in each abbreviated word. Also, use capital letters where they belong.

thursday, september 13, 2001 → Thurs., Sept. 13, 2001
wednesday, november 7, 2001 → Wed., Nov. 7, 2001
monday, february 18, 2002 → Mon., Feb. 18, 2002
saturday, august 17, 2002 → Sat., Aug. 17, 2002
tuesday, january 22, 2001 → Tues., Jan. 22, 2001
friday, april 19, 2002 → Fri., Apr. 19, 2002
sunday, may 6, 2001 → Sun., May 6, 2001

There is an even shorter way to write dates. Use numbers! 8/4/01 means August 4, 2001. The months of the year, beginning with January are numbered 1 to 12. Number the months on the left. Then try the shortest way to write the dates below.

1 January
2 February
3 March
4 April
5 May
6 June
7 July
8 August
9 September
10 October
11 November
12 December

Aug. 16, 2001 → 8/16/01
Oct. 31, 2001 → 10/31/01
Dec. 25, 2001 → 12/25/01
Mar. 4, 2002 → 3/4/02

Apostrophes in Possessives

An apostrophe followed by an **s** is used to show that someone owns something. Just add an apostrophe when the owner's name ends with an **s**.

Tiger's team is playing Malcolm's team.

Note: When two or more people own something you just add an apostrophe.

All of the players' bats are made of wood.

Add 's to each critter's name to show that he or she owns something.

Little Critter's hat

Malcolm's lunchbox

Gator's backpack

Gabby's book

Label the pictures below. Look at page 4 to help you spell the names.

Maurice's picture

Bun Bun's carrot

Tiger's shoe

Use the pictures above and on page 50 to help you write two sentences to show ownership. Don't forget to use 's in each sentence.

Example: Tiger's shoe is blue.

1. Sentences will vary.

2.

Handwriting Check

Look at your handwriting above. Are your words sitting on the line? Did you take your time and use your best handwriting? Did you put spaces between your words? Do your tall letters touch the top line and your small letters fit between the dotted and the lower lines?

How did you do? (circle one)

Great!

Good!

O.K.

I'll do better next time.

Underlining Titles

Underline the titles of books and movies when you are writing their names. Think of the line as a shelf and pretend you are putting the book on a shelf.

Little Critter loves to visit the library. His favorite books are The Wizard of Oz and Just So Stories.

Read each sentence below. Underline each title.

1. Bat Child is reading 101 Knock-Knock Jokes to Amuse Your Friends.
2. The Carrot Seed is Bun Bun's favorite book.
3. Maurice and Molly just finished reading Double Trouble.
4. In the spring Grandma Critter read Grow Your Own Vegetable Soup.

Read each sentence below. Underline the four book and movie titles.

1. After Little Sister read Peter Pan, she wished she could fly to Never-Never Land.
2. Little Critter and his friends went to see the movie The Further Adventures of Super Critter ten times.
3. Gabby gave Gator the book Treasure Island for his birthday.

4. Molly said that The Wind in the Willows is her favorite book.

Write two sentences about your favorite book and movie. Don't forget to underline the titles.

1. Sentences will vary.

2.

Challenge: Make a list of all the books you read in one month. Record the titles in a notebook. Remember to underline the titles. Next month, try to read even more books!

Review: Punctuation

Read the story below. Circle the set of words in the sentences where quotation marks should be used.

Little Critter asked, Mom, can I take the recycling down to the market? Sure, That would be a big help, replied Mom. Little Critter stopped to get the mail on his way out. Hey Mom! I got a letter, he yelled.

Who is it from? asked Mom.

It is an invitation to a costume party.

Yippee! yelled Little Critter.

Maybe you can look for costume ideas when you are in town, said Dad.

That is a great idea. Bye! said Little Critter.

Write the abbreviations.

Please come to my costume party!

When: 3:00 on Sat. (Saturday), Oct. (October) 27th

Where: 26 Critterville St. (Street)

Read the following paragraph. Find book titles and underline them.

Little Critter stopped by Gator's house on the way into town. Gator had received an invitation from Gabby, too. They decided to go to the library to get some books about costumes. Gator checked out Creative Costumes. Little Critter checked out Fabulous Costumes Without Sewing and Crazy Costumes You Can Make. Then they headed to the market.

Show ownership by adding an apostrophe and an s ('s) to a name. Write the names so that they show ownership.

Little Critter and Gator walked to Mr. Molini's (Mr. Molini) Market. They walked past Hogley's (Hogley) Hardware. After they dropped the recycling off at the market, they decided to take the long way home. They walked past the pet store, the pond, and the zoo. Little Critter bought a yo-yo at Stork's (Stork) Toy Shop. He tried it out as they walked to Mrs. Castle's (Mrs. Castle) Costume Shop. Inside they found some great costume ideas for Gabby's (Gabby) party. Finally, they headed home. They were ready to make their costumes. What do you think they decided to be? Answers will vary.

Verbs – Has, Have

A verb is a word that tells what the subject of the sentence does.

Use has when you are talking about one subject.

Little Sister has a shadow.

Use have when you are talking about yourself or more than one subject.

I have a shadow.
My friends have shadows, too.

Little Sister wrote a story about her shadow. Read the sentences below. Fill in each blank with **has** or **have**.

I have a shy shadow. I think it has a hiding place. It also has many shapes. I have only one shape. My shadow and I have a good time together.

This letter has five mistakes. Draw a line through each incorrect word. Write the correct word above it. When you are done, read the letter aloud to be sure it makes sense.

Example: The teams ~~has~~ have colorful uniforms.

May 10, 2001

Dear Grandma,

I am on a t-ball team. It ~~have~~ has 10 players. Our uniforms are cool. We have red shirts and white pants. The red shirts ~~has~~ have blue numbers on them. Mine ~~have~~ has a number 6 on it. We ~~has~~ have a game on Saturday. I ~~has~~ have butterflies in my stomach. Wish me luck.

Love,
Little Sister

Write one sentence about something you have. Write another sentence about something a friend has.

1. Sentences will vary.

2.

Verbs – Is, Are

Is and are are verbs. They tell what the subject of the sentence is.

Use is when you are talking about one subject.

Malcolm is always doing something funny.

Use are when you are talking about more than one subject.

Little Critter and Gabby are funny, too.

Read the sentences below. Fill in each blank with **is** or **are**.

Little Critter and Gabby are being silly.

So is Malcolm. He is acting like a

creature from outer space. They are all waiting

for the bus. I think it is time for the bus to come.

This paragraph has six mistakes. Draw a line through each incorrect word. Write the correct word above it. When you are done, read the sentences aloud to be sure they make sense.

Example: The children ~~is~~ are in the park.

Tiger and Gator ~~is~~ are at the park. They ~~is~~ are waiting for their friends. Little Critter ~~are~~ is coming on the bus. Gabby and Malcolm ~~is~~ are coming with him. Tiger ~~are~~ is looking down the street. He sees the bus two blocks away. His friends ~~is~~ are on their way.

Write one sentence about your friend. Write another sentence about the two of you. Use **is** in one sentence and **are** in the other one.

1. Sentences will vary.

2.

Verbs – Was, Were

Was and were are used to tell something that happened in the past. Note: Use were with the word you.

Use was when you are talking about one person.

Little Critter was hurrying to school.

Use were when you are talking about more than one person or thing.

They were hurrying to school.

Fill in the blanks with **was** or **were**.

Little Critter was in a hurry. He had to go back home and get his lunchbox. Maurice and Molly were in a hurry, too. They overslept and were late. It was not a good way to start the day. Luckily, they made it to school on time. They were not late.

This story has four mistakes. Draw a line through each incorrect word. Write the correct word above it.

Example: We ~~was~~ were on time.

Malcolm was in the lunchroom. His lunch ~~were~~ was at home on the kitchen counter. His grandma ~~were~~ was at work. Malcolm ~~were~~ was hungry. Little Critter shared his lunch. Then Malcolm ~~were~~ was not hungry anymore.

Write two sentences telling about what happened when you forgot something. Use **was** or **were** in each sentence.

1. Sentences will vary.

2.

Handwriting Check

Look at your handwriting above. Are your words sitting on the line? Did you take your time and use your best handwriting? Did you put spaces between your words? Do your tall letters touch the top line and your small letters fit between the dotted and the lower lines?

How did you do? (circle one)

Great!

Good!

O.K.

I'll do better next time.

Verbs – Ran, Run

Ran and run are forms of the verb to run.

Use ran alone.

I ran as fast as I could.
My dog ran behind me.

Use run with has or have.

I have run with my dog.
Blue has run along with me.

Read the sentences. Write **ran** or **run** in each blank.

Tiger has run many races.

Little Critter and Gator have run many races with him.

Tiger ran faster than everybody else.

Tiger ran faster than the wind.

There are five mistakes in this paragraph. Draw a line through each incorrect word. Write the correct word above it.

Example: The boy has ~~ran~~ run after the ball.

Gator ~~run~~ ran across the basketball court. Tiger and Gabby ~~run~~ ran to block him. They have ~~ran~~ run to block him before. But Gator is a good basketball player. He throws the ball. It goes through the hoop. Now Little Critter has ~~ran~~ run onto the court. He will take Gator's place. Gator has ~~ran~~ run enough for a while.

Think about animals, people, and things that run. Write one sentence using **ran**. Write another using **has run** or **have run**.

1. Sentences will vary.

2.

Challenge: Clocks run, fans run, and children run to have fun! Make a list of all the things that run. Walk around the house to help you come up with ideas.

Review: Verbs

Read the sentences. Write **is** or **are** in each blank.

It is fall. Little Critter and Little Sister are happy. They are going to pick apples. It is fun. It is also hard work, because the apples are heavy.

Read the sentences. Write **was** or **were** in each blank.

The leaves were all over the yard. Little Critter raked them into a big pile. Little Sister was there. She was helping. When Little Critter finished, they ran toward the pile. The pile was high. Little Critter and Little Sister jumped in the leaves.

Read this paragraph. Look for **has** and **have**. If the word is used incorrectly, draw a line through it. Write the correct word above it.

I ~~has~~ have four apples. Little Sister ~~have~~ has three apples. Together we have enough to make a pie. Mom ~~have~~ has a good recipe for apple pie. We ~~has~~ have fun making a yummy dessert for dinner.

Read the sentences below. If the underlined word is incorrect, draw a line through it. Write the correct word above it.

Grandpa has an old clock in the hall. It has ~~ran~~ run for a hundred years. He has a car and a tractor. They have ~~ran~~ run for thirty years. He has a dog and a cat. They have ~~ran~~ run for ten years. The dog ran after the cat. The cat ~~run~~ ran after a mouse and the mouse ~~run~~ ran up the clock.

Verbs – Did, Done

Did and done are forms of the verb to do.

Use did alone.

I did my homework.
Gator did his, too.

Use done with has or have.

I have done all my homework.
Gator has done his, too.

Gator made a list of all the things he accomplished this week. Review his list below. If the underlined word is used incorrectly, draw a line through it. Write the correct word above it.

- ☐ I did the dishes.
- ☐ I ~~done~~ did the yard work.
- ☐ I have ~~did~~ done the vacuuming.
- ☐ I have done my laundry.
- ☐ I ~~done~~ did my paper route.

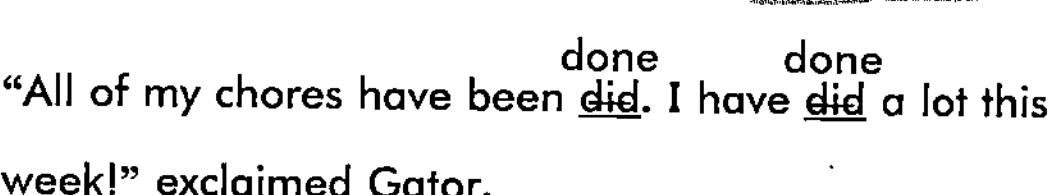

"All of my chores have been ~~did~~ done. I have ~~did~~ done a lot this week!" exclaimed Gator.

This report has four mistakes. Draw a line through each incorrect word. Write the correct word above it.

Example: We ~~done~~ did a good job.

The members of the Critterville Nature Club ~~done~~ did something for their town. They cleaned up the park. They have ~~did~~ done some hiking and exploring together, but this was different. They ~~done~~ did a great job picking up litter. Gabby made a No Littering poster. Tiger and Little Critter painted the trash cans. The Nature Club has ~~did~~ done a lot of good things to make Critterville Park a nice place.

Think about a chore you or your friends have done. Write two sentences about it. Be sure to use **did, have done,** or **has done** in each sentence.

1. Sentences will vary.

2.

Verbs – Went, Gone

Went and gone are forms of the verb to go.

Use went alone.

Malcolm went to the carnival.

Use gone with has or have.

Little Critter has gone to the carnival, too.

Read the sentences. Write **went** or **gone** in each blank.

Little Critter went to the carnival. His family has gone every year. First, he went in the Fun House. Next he went on the Ferris Wheel. Then he went on all the other rides. He and his sister have gone on all the rides before, but they love to go again and again.

This paragraph has four mistakes. Draw a line through each incorrect word. Write the correct word above it.

Example: My sister has ~~went~~ gone to school.

Dad and I went to a soccer game. Gabby has ~~went~~ gone with us. We have ~~went~~ gone to pick up Gator and Tiger. Malcolm has ~~went~~ gone ahead. He has ~~went~~ gone to buy tickets. His grandma went with him.

Write two sentences about a time you went somewhere. Be sure to use **went, has gone,** or **have gone** in each sentence.

1. Sentences will vary.

2.

Verbs – Saw, Seen

Saw and seen are forms of the verb to see.

Use saw alone.

I saw a picture of the Grand Canyon.

Use seen with has or have.

Dad has seen the Grand Canyon in real life.

Read the sentences. Write **saw** or **seen** in each blank.

The Critter family was going on a trip. Little Critter and Little Sister were very excited because they had never seen the Grand Canyon before. On the way they saw a sign for the World's Largest Ball of String. They also saw a lot of corn fields. They drove for hours and hours. "Has anyone seen the map?" asked Dad. "Dad, I saw a sign for the Grand Canyon. It is only 10 miles away," said Little Critter. "Good job, Little Critter," said Dad. Finally, they arrived at the Grand Canyon. "I have never seen anything like it," said Little Critter.

Little Critter's postcard has two mistakes. Draw a line through each incorrect word. Write the correct word above it.

Example: We ~~seen~~ saw a bear in the woods.

August 1, 2002

Dear Maurice and Molly,

We are having fun on our trip. I ~~seen~~ saw giant sequoia trees. They are taller than buildings. I never ~~seen~~ saw anything like them before. I wish you were here.

From,
Little Critter

Maurice and Molly
22 Foxtail Road
Critterville, U.S.A.

Write two sentences about something you have seen. Remember to use **saw**, **has seen**, or **have seen** in each sentence.

1. Sentences will vary.

2.

Verbs – Came, Come

Came and come are forms of the verb to come.

Use came alone.

Everyone came to Gabby's party in a costume.

Use come with has or have.
Use has come with one subject.

Bun Bun has come dressed as a ballerina.

Use have come when you talk about more then one subject.

Maurice and Molly have come dressed as a pair of mittens.

Fill in each blank with **came** or **come**.

- Little Critter came early to help Gabby set up.
- Malcolm has come dressed as a pirate.
- Gator and Tiger have come as storybook characters.
- Gabby is glad all of her friends came to the party.

After the party, Gabby wrote a note to Bun Bun. There are some mistakes in this letter. Draw a line through each incorrect word. Write the correct word above it.

November 1, 2001

Dear Bun Bun,

I am glad you ~~come~~ came to my party. I have ~~came~~ come to all of your parties. Thank you for bringing cookies. I didn't know you made them. I thought they ~~come~~ came from the store.

Your friend,
Gabby

Note: **Come** can be used by itself when you are asking someone to come with you to a party or event.

Example: Please come to the library with me.

Write two sentences asking someone to come with you somewhere.

1. Sentences will vary.

2.

Review: Verbs

Read the sentences. Write **came** or **come** in each blank.

The sea came to the beach yesterday.

It has come again today.

Do you think it came to find a shell?

Maybe it has come with a tale to tell.

Read Little Critter's story below. Write **saw** or **seen** in each blank.

I went to the circus. I saw a clown riding a mule.

Then I noticed something funny. I saw two monkeys riding on the clown. I have not seen that before! Then I saw dogs riding on each of the monkeys. Did you see eight fleas riding on each of the dogs?

Challenge: How many things were riding on the mule? Don't forget to count the monkeys, dogs, and fleas.

Read the story below. Choose the correct word and write it in the blank.

Little Sister has gone (went, gone) to the park. She wants to climb on the monkey bars. Gabby and Little Critter went (went, gone) with her. They have gone (went, gone) to slide and swing. Little Sister did (did, done) it. She climbed to the top of the monkey bars. Oh, no! What has she done (did, done)! She can't get down. Little Critter went (went, gone) to help her. He has done (did, done) a very nice thing. What a thoughtful big brother.

Look at the words in each column. Draw a line between pairs that make sense. Use each pair only once. Answers may vary.

Maurice and Molly have	went to see the movie star.
My brother	ran to get the mail.
Gabby	gone to feed the ducks.
Little Sister has	come home early today.
Bat Child	run in a race.
I think Tiger has	came to the park with us.

Adjectives That Compare

We can use words to describe and compare things. Add -er to an adjective when you compare two things. Add -est when you compare three or more things.

Little Critter is **fast**.
Gabby is **faster**.
Tiger is the **fastest**.

This chart is not finished. Fill in the empty boxes with the correct word.

fast	faster	fastest
short	shorter	shortest
large	larger	largest
bright	brighter	brightest
long	longer	longest
high	higher	highest

Tiger's report has four mistakes. Draw a line through each incorrect word. Write the correct word above it.

Example: Maurice is ~~shortest~~ shorter than Tiger.

A gorilla is big. A chimp is ~~smallest~~ smaller than a gorilla. A baboon is smart. A gorilla is ~~smart~~ smarter than a baboon. Did you know that a baboon is a monkey, not an ape? Someone ~~old~~ older than I am told me that. Apes are smarter than monkeys and chimps are the ~~smarter~~ smartest of the apes.

Use the words from the chart on page 76 to compare something. Write two sentences. Be sure to write complete sentences, like the ones below.

Little Critter is **taller** than Little Sister.
Malcolm is the **tallest** boy in the class.

1. Sentences will vary.

2.

Homophones – To, Too, Two

Some words sound alike even when they mean different things and have different spellings. These words are called homophones.

The word to has two meanings. It can mean "toward." To is also used before a verb.

I found a penny when I walked to the store.
I want to read that book.

The word too has two meanings. It can mean "also." Too can also be used to mean "very" or "more than enough."

My brother found a penny, too.
I am too tired to watch the movie.

The word two means the number 2.

Bun Bun found two pennies.

Read Little Sister's paragraph below. Fill in each blank with **to**, **too**, or **two**.

My brother is learning to juggle. He started with two balls. I asked him to teach me, too.

Little Critter's diary entry has four mistakes. Draw a line through each incorrect word. Write the correct word above it.

Example: I'm not ~~to~~ too sleepy.

Maurice and Molly asked me to come ~~too~~ to their house after school. They are going ~~two~~ to have ~~to~~ two kinds of snacks. Tiger is coming.

Gabby isn't coming. She is ~~to~~ too busy.

Write two sentences. One should be about two of something. The other should tell about going to a place you like. Try to use too in one of the sentences, too!

1. Sentences will vary.

2.

Challenge: Here are some other homophones. Read them to someone and talk about their different meanings. Can you think of any others?

one/won	sun/son	new/knew	for/four
your/you're	ate/eight	read/red	know/no
meet/meat	blew/blue	their/there/they're	

Review: Adjectives That Compare, Homophones

Fill in the empty boxes to complete the chart.

slow	slower	slowest
fast	faster	fastest
dark	darker	darkest
little	littler	littlest
tall	taller	tallest
short	shorter	shortest

Read the poem below. Write **to**, **too**, or **two** in each blank.

This morning it started to rain.
The two of us were sad.
We couldn't go to the soccer game.
"That's too bad," said Dad.

Finish the comparisons by writing the correct word in each blank.

1. Little Critter is older than Little Sister. (old, older, oldest)

2. Little Sister is the youngest member of the family. (young, younger, youngest)

3. Dad is taller than Mom. (tall, taller, tallest)

4. Mom's ice cream cone is the biggest. (big, bigger, biggest)

5. Little Critter's ice cream is melting the fastest. (fast, faster, fastest)

6. The sun is hot. (hot, hotter, hottest)

Plurals That Add -s

Nouns are words that name objects. You can make most nouns mean "more than one" by adding **-s** to the end of the word. This is called a plural noun.

one shoe	two shoes
one ball	five balls

Write each word so that it means more than one.

1. animal	animals	6. bat	bats
2. sister	sisters	7. book	books
3. kitten	kittens	8. toy	toys
4. truck	trucks	9. dog	dogs
5. backpack	backpacks	10. river	rivers

There are three mistakes in Tiger's invitation. Draw a line through each incorrect word. Write the correct word above it.

Example: I saw two ~~dog~~ dogs.

Please come to my birthday party!
We will play ~~game~~ games and have fun. We will eat hot ~~dog~~ dogs and potato ~~chip~~ chips. The party will last two hours. Hope you can come!

Fill in the blanks to make a list about the picture above. Use the words to write two sentences about the picture.

one	cake	two	balloons
three	presents	eight	candles

1. Sentences will vary.

2.

Plurals That Add -es

To make some nouns mean more than one, you add **-es**. Add **-es** to words ending in **sh**, **ch**, **x**, **s**, and **z**.

one bush	two bushes
one lunch	two lunches
one fox	two foxes
one bus	two buses
one quiz.	two quizes

Write each word so that it means more than one.

1. brush	brushes	6. dress	dresses
2. ax	axes	7. flash	flashes
3. box	boxes	8. lunch	lunches
4. bench	benches	9. dish	dishes
5. class	classes	10. bunch	bunches

Fill in each blank with the correct plural by adding **-s** or **-es** to the word below each line.

Maurice and Molly went to the Critterville Zoo. They saw zebras (zebra) and lions (lion). They ate their lunches (lunch) on a couple of benches (bench). In the petting zoo, they touched snakes (snake), goats (goat) and baby foxes (fox). The seals made a lot of splashes (splash). Wow! Did the twins (twin) get wet!

Choose two words that mean more than one from the list on page 84. Use each word in a sentence.

1. Sentences will vary.

2.

Review: Plurals

Add **-s** to make each word mean "more than one." Write the word on the line.

1. ball  balls
2. bat bats
3. shoe shoes
4. glove gloves
5. field fields

Add **-es** to make each word mean "more than one." Write the word on the line.

1. brush brushes
2. box boxes
3. wish wishes
4. mess messes
5. branch branches

Fill in the blanks by adding -s or -es to the word below each line.

1. Grandma sent me a box of paints (paint).
2. She also sent two new brushes (brush).
3. My sister got ten markers (marker).
4. We made a lot of pictures (picture).
5. We made a lot of messes (mess), too.
6. I am sending two paintings (painting) to Grandma.
7. One is a boy holding two bunches (bunch) of flowers.
8. One is a girl and a boy on their bikes (bike).

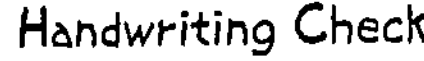

Look at your handwriting above. Are your words sitting on the line? Did you take your time and use your best handwriting? Did you put spaces between your words? Do your tall letters touch the top line and your small letters fit between the dotted and the lower lines?

How did you do? (circle one)

Great!

Good!

O.K.

I'll do better next time.

Contractions

Sometimes we put two words together to make one shorter word. The shorter word is called a contraction. An apostrophe (') is put in the place of the letters that are left out when two words are put together.

is not = isn't
are not = aren't
we will = we'll
they are = they're

Look at the words in the first column. Circle the correct contraction in the same row.

cannot	cann't	cant'	(can't)
it is	(it's)	itis	its'
did not	(didn't)	din't	didnt
I am	I'am	(I'm)	Im'
I will	Iw'll	(I'll)	Ill
we are	we'ere	w're	(we're)
you are	(you're)	y'ar	youer
I have	I'ave	(I've)	Ih've
she would	(she'd)	shewo'd	shel'l

Write the correct contraction in each blank.

1. Little Sister didn't (didn't, don't) want to clean her room.
2. Little Critter said he'd (he'd, she'd) help her.
3. "Maybe I'll (I'll, I'm) find my fishing pole, he told her.
4. "I don't (didn't, don't) have any of your stuff," said Little Sister.

Fill in the blanks with the correct contraction.

I'm (I am) helping Little Sister clean her room. First, I'll (I will) look in her closet. It's (It is) a real mess in there. I can't (cannot) believe my eyes. Look at all this stuff she borrowed from me. I've (I have) a feeling my fishing pole is in there, too.

Isn't, Aren't

Isn't and aren't are contractions.

Use isn't when you talk about one

Little Critter isn't playing ball.

Use aren't when you talk about more than one.

Gabby and Tiger aren't playing ball, either.

Read the story below. Write **isn't** or **aren't** in the blanks.

Little Critter isn't eating his peas. He put them in the flowerpot. Mom saw him. Peas aren't part of her ivy plant. Then Little Critter tried to make Blue eat his peas. Blue isn't happy. I hope Little Critter's peas aren't about to land on my plate!

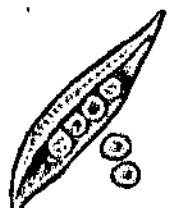

Read Gabby's paragraph about four animals she saw at the zoo. Draw a line through each incorrect word. Write the correct word above it. There are three mistakes.

Example: That book ~~aren't~~ isn't about snakes.

Seals and sea lions can swim but they ~~isn't~~ aren't fish. A bat can fly but it ~~isnt~~ isn't a bird. An armadillo is covered with bony plates but it ~~aren't~~ isn't a reptile. Seals, sea lions, bats, and armadillos are all mammals.

Write two sentences about animals that are different. Use **isn't** and **aren't**.

Example: Zebras and giraffes aren't the same. A zebra isn't as tall as a giraffe.

1. Sentences will vary.

2.

Wasn't, Weren't

Wasn't and weren't are two more contractions.

Use wasn't when you talk about one

Gabby wasn't at the clubhouse.

Use weren't when you talk about more than one and with the word you.

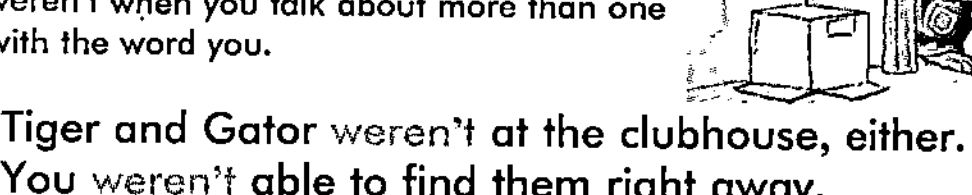

Tiger and Gator weren't at the clubhouse, either. You weren't able to find them right away.

Read this paragraph that Little Critter's mom wrote about him. She left out the words **wasn't** and **weren't**. Write the correct word in each blank.

You were looking for your friends. They weren't playing ball. Tiger wasn't at the karate school. Gabby wasn't at the library. Gator wasn't in his backyard. Weren't you surprised to find them at your house, looking for you?

Bun Bun's thank you note has three mistakes. Draw a line through each incorrect word. Write the correct word above it.

Example: You ~~wasn't~~ weren't late.

Dear Mrs. Critter,

Thank you for taking me to the circus. ~~Weren't~~ Wasn't it fun? I ~~weren't~~ wasn't really scared. I knew those two acrobats weren't going to fall. You ~~wasn't~~ weren't scared, were you?

Love,

Bun Bun

Write two sentences. Use **wasn't** or **weren't** in each sentence.

Example: The car **wasn't** big. The clowns **weren't** happy.

1. Sentences will vary.

2.

Review: Contractions

Draw lines from the words in the left column to the contractions in the right column.

cannot	I've
did not	didn't
I am	can't
we are	we're
I have	isn't
is not	you're
do not	it's
I will	they'll
you are	don't
it is	I'm
they will	I'll

Read the story below. Fill in the blanks with **isn't** or **aren't**.

My dog Blue isn't a collie. He isn't a husky, either. My mom and dad aren't sure what he is. Blue likes to play in the mud. He can get really dirty. Unfortunately, baths aren't his favorite thing.

Here are some contractions. Write them as two words.

she'll	→	she	will	that's	→	that	is
he's	→	he	is	he'd	→	he	would
hasn't	→	has	not	I've	→	I	have
doesn't	→	does	not	they're	→	they	are

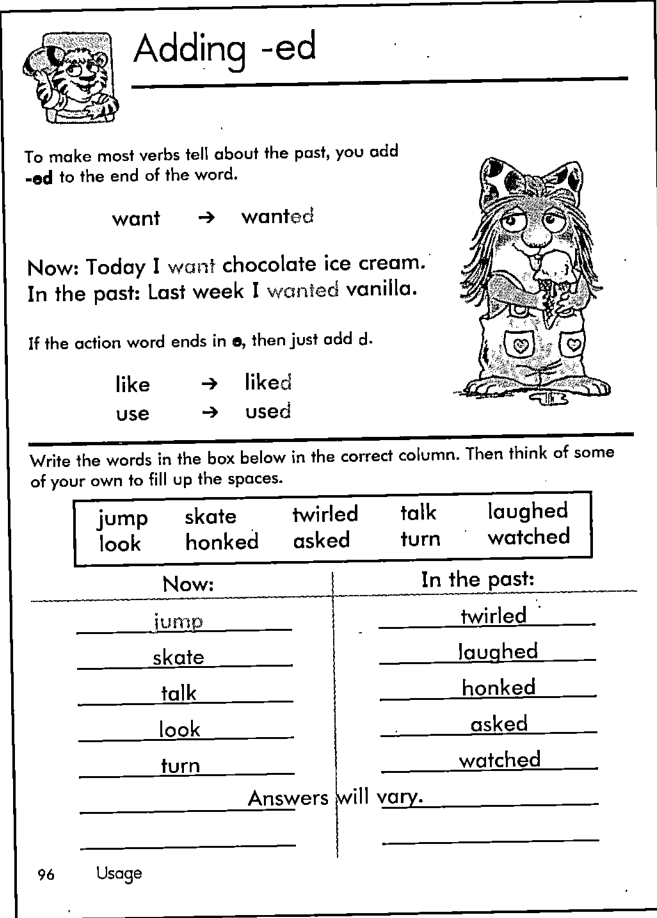

Adding -ed

To make most verbs tell about the past, you add **-ed** to the end of the word.

want → wanted

Now: Today I want chocolate ice cream.
In the past: Last week I wanted vanilla.

If the action word ends in **e**, then just add d.

like → liked
use → used

Write the words in the box below in the correct column. Then think of some of your own to fill up the spaces.

jump	skate	twirled	talk	laughed
look	honked	asked	turn	watched

Now:	In the past:
jump	twirled
skate	laughed
talk	honked
look	asked
turn	watched
Answers will vary.	

Fill in the blanks with the verb that shows that the action happened in the past.

1. Little Critter kicked (kick, kicked) the ball to Tiger.
2. Little Sister wanted (want, wanted) to play, too.
3. Little Critter and Tiger called (call, called) to her.
4. Little Sister rushed (rush, rushed) over.
5. They all played (play, played) ball.

Write two sentences about something you did last week. Use action words with **-ed** on the end.

Example: Little Sister and I **played** in the rain.

1. Sentences will vary.

2.

Review: Adding -ed, -s

Fill in each blank. Show that the action happened in the past.

1. Last week, Malcolm played his old toy drum. (play)
2. He banged on it with a wooden spoon. (bang)
3. The neighbors covered their ears. (cover)
4. Malcolm's grandma closed the window. (close)

Fill in each blank. Show that the action happened in the past.

1. Little Critter hunted for his homework. (hunt)
2. He poked around in his closet. (poke)
3. He reached under the couch. (reach)
4. Then he chased his dog Blue. (chase)

Choose the correct form of the verb. Write your answer in each blank. Read each sentence aloud to see if it sounds right.

1. Gabby lives next door to Little Critter. (live, lives)
2. Gator cleaned his room. (clean, cleaned)
3. Bat Child tells jokes and loves to do magic tricks. (tell, tells) (love, loves)
4. Miss Kitty works at Critterville Elementary. (work, works)

These are Little Sister's directions for making breakfast. Look at the underlined words. If the wrong verb is used, cross it out. Write the correct verb above it. There are five mistakes. Read the sentences aloud to help you find the mistakes.

First you ~~opens~~ open the box. Then you ~~pours~~ pour out the cereal. Oops, I forgot. You need a bowl. My big brother ~~add~~ adds milk for me. Sometimes, I ~~spills~~ spill the milk when I pour it. Then I ~~eats~~ eat my breakfast.

Using I

When you talk about what you do or who you are, use the word I.

Always write I with a capital letter. I is a pronoun that is used as a subject.

I helped my mom today.

When you talk about yourself and someone else, speak of yourself last.

Yes: Mom and I planted flowers.
No: I and Mom planted flowers.

Help Little Critter finish this story. Write I in the blanks. Then read each sentence to a friend.

Mom asked me to show her how a robot acts. I marched across the room. Then she asked me to work hard like a robot. I put my toys away. I also gave Mom my dirty shirts and socks. I think Mom tricked me into cleaning my room!

Little Critter's journal entry has three mistakes. Cross out each mistake. Write the correct word or words above it.

Example: Mom and ~~me~~ I ate breakfast.

~~I and Dad~~ Dad and I were busy today. We worked outside. ~~i~~ I pulled weeds and planted flowers. Gabby came over. Dad, Gabby, and I watered the new plants. Gabby and ~~i~~ I got dirty. I had lots of fun.

Write two sentences to tell about something you and someone else did.

1. Sentences will vary.

2.

Handwriting Check

Look at your handwriting above. Are your words sitting on the line? Did you take your time and use your best handwriting? Did you put spaces between your words? Do your tall letters touch the top line and your small letters fit between the dotted and the lower lines?

How did you do? (circle one)

Great!

Good!

O.K.

I'll do better next time.

Using Me

Sometimes when you talk about yourself, you are not the main person the sentence is about. In this case, use the word me.
Me is a pronoun, just like **I** is.

Mom walked with me to the pool.

When you talk about yourself and someone else, speak of yourself last.

Little Critter came with Mom and me.

Fill in each blank with the correct word or words.

1. My brother chased __me__ (I, me) through the house.
2. He wanted __me__ (I, me) to leave him alone.
3. Mom told __Little Critter and me__ (me and Little Critter, Little Critter and me) to stop running through the house.
4. So I ran outside, and Little Critter kept chasing __me__ (I, me)!

Find the four mistakes in this story. Draw a line through the incorrect word or words. Write the correct word or words above them.

Example: They were waiting for ~~me and Bun Bun~~ Bun Bun and me.

Dad and I have a secret. It is just between Dad and ~~I~~ me. Dad told it to ~~I~~ me last night. He said he knew I would not tell. He said it was only for ~~me and him~~ him and me. Mom wants ~~me and Dad~~ Dad and me to tell her the secret. We can't! The secret is about Mom's birthday present.

Write two sentences about times when someone did something for you. Be sure to use **me** in each one.

1. Sentences will vary.
2.

Review: I, Me

Read this paragraph. Write **I** or **me** in each blank.

Gabby and __I__ went to Snow Hill. She and __I__ wanted to go sledding. Gabby went first. Then she gave the sled to __me__. She waited for me at the bottom of the hill. Next, she and __I__ rode on the sled together. The sled went very fast with both Gabby and __me__ on it.

Find the three mistakes in this story. Draw a line through the incorrect word. Write the correct word above it.

Example: He called ~~I~~ me on the phone.

~~Me~~ I like to sleep with my teddy bear. He makes me feel safe at night. The dark does not bother ~~I~~ me when Teddy is watching. I don't tell my friends about my teddy. I think they might laugh. Dad told ~~I~~ me he used to sleep with a teddy bear.

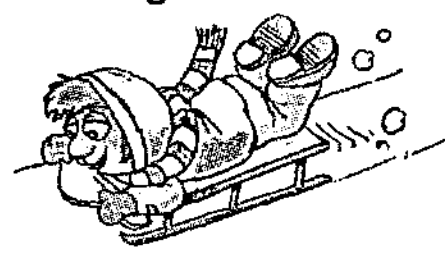

Read each sentence. Choose the correct answer and write it in the blank.

1. Both __Dad and I__ (Dad and me, Dad and I) wanted to go to the library.
2. __I__ (I, me) needed a book for a book report.
3. Little Sister wanted to come with __Dad and me__ (Dad and me, Dad and I).
4. __Little Sister and I__ (Little Sister and I, Little Sister and me) went to the children's section.
5. I found the book __I__ (I, me) needed.
6. Dad helped __me__ (I, me) check it out.
7. __I__ (I, me) ran to the car with my book.
8. Little Sister ran behind __me__ (I, me).

Rhyming Words

Rhyming words are very helpful when you want to write poetry and songs, or when you want to add interest to stories you write.

Read the poem. Circle the rhyming words.

Mr. Rubble is a (man)
Who collects a lot of (things)
Like buoy bells, an old tin (can,)
A smelly sock, and mattress (springs.)

Do you need a broken (clock?)
Rusty rings? Some oyster (shells?)
A frying pan? A cinder (block?)
Mr. Rubble buys and (sells)

Challenge: Look for other poems in this workbook. Find all of the rhyming words that you can.

The rhyming words from the poem on page 106 are listed below. Add your own rhyming words to each list. Sample answers are given.

sock/clock/block	pan/can/man
lock	fan
knock	plan
rock	van
dock	ran

things/springs/rings	bells/shells/sells
brings	smells
sings	tells
dings	yells
strings	spells

Bat Child wants to tell you about himself in some rhymes he wrote. Help him finish each rhyme by filling in the blank with a word that rhymes with the word in red. Sample answers given.

My name is Bat Child. I'm a funny guy,
My favorite dessert is mosquito pie.

I have a little sister named Baby Bat,
She likes to torment our dear, old cat.

I'm a magician if you didn't know,
So have a seat and enjoy the show.

Abracadabra-Kalamaroo,
Let's disappear and go to the zoo.

Compound Words

A compound word is a **big** word made up of **two** smaller words. Write the compound word for each picture below

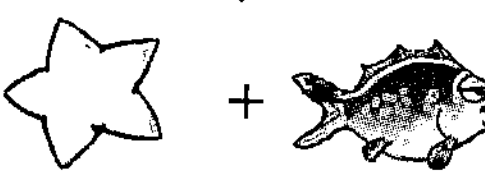 starfish	 doorbell
toothbrush	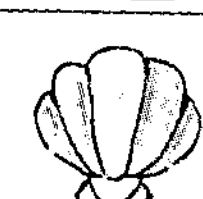 eggshell
pancake	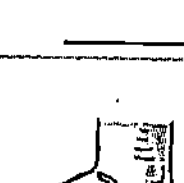  football
doghouse	sunflower

Tiger got his compound words a little mixed up. Circle the incorrect words. Rewrite each sentence with the correct compound word from the box below.

snowball	driveway	football	sunburn

1. We had a (snowflake) fight last winter.
   We had a snowball fight last winter.
2. I got a (sunrise) at the beach.
   I got a sunburn at the beach.
3. We played basketball on the (runway.)
   We played basketball on the driveway.
4. I threw the (footprints) as hard as I could down the field.
   I threw the football as hard as I could down the field.

Challenge: Make a list of all the compound words you can think of. Ask friends and family to help you. Keep your list below.

Answers will vary.

Common Nouns

Nouns are parts of speech. A common noun names any person, place, or thing.

Person	Place	Thing
teacher	school	pencil
baby	park	bottle

Make a list of all the common nouns you can find in the picture. Put them in the correct column. Sample answers given.

Person	Place	Thing
police officer	sewer	stairs
boy	street	book
critters	pond	grass
children	school	trash can
girl	library	bus
teacher	playground	chicken

Read the paragraph below. Write a common noun in each blank. Sample answers given.

I really wanted a new game. I asked my dad whether I could have one. I had to earn money. I made rings and sold them. I cleaned the house. Finally I went to the store and bought a game with the money I earned.

Write a sentence about a pet. Underline the common nouns.
Sample answers given

My puppy ate dinner.

Reread your sentence. Change some of the common nouns to make the sentence funny. Rewrite the sentence.

My puppy ate my shoe.

Using **a** and **an**

The words a and an help point out a noun. Use a before consonant sounds. Use an before vowel sounds.

a	b	c	d	e	f	g	h	i	j	k	l	m
n	o	p	q	r	s	t	u	v	w	x	y	z

Examples:

an **apple**	a **banana**
an **egg**	a **chicken**
an **insect**	a **fish**
an **octopus**	a **raindrop**
an **umbrella**	a **snowflake**

Little Critter is packing for a trip! Look in his suitcase to see what he packed. Make a list of all the things he packed. Use **a** or **an** in your list. Circle the thing he probably shouldn't have packed. Sample answers given.

- a toothbrush
- a comb
- a teddy bear
- an orange
- a map
- a toy airplane
- a shirt
- a sweater
- an umbrella
- (an ant farm)

Fill in the blanks with **a** or **an**.

Mom sent Little Critter to Molini's Market to buy a loaf of bread, an onion, and a quart of milk. When he got there he forgot what mom wanted. He bought an apple, a box of cookies, and a quart of orange juice. When he got home, he showed Mom the groceries. She sent Little Critter back to the store. This time she gave him a list.

Look at all the things around you. Make a list of things you see. Place them in the appropriate column.

a	an
Answers will vary.	

Common and Proper Nouns

A common noun names any person, place, or thing.

A proper noun names a special person, a special place, or a special thing. A proper noun begins with a capital letter.

Mr. Molini lives in the town of Critterville.

Place each word in the word bank in the correct column. Fill the blanks with words of your own.

Word Bank

Critterville	ball	Texas	library
boat	Little Sister	road	Main Street
Canada	town	country	Hogley's Hardware
Molini's Market	boy	Gabby	mountain

proper nouns	common nouns
Critterville	ball
Canada	boat
Molini's Market	town
Little Sister	boy
Texas	road
Gabby	country
Main Street	library
Hogley's Hardware	mountain

Read the paragraph below. Write a proper noun in each blank.

Sample answer given.

My name is Little Critter. I am on a secret mission to find out why all the students at Critterville School in Critterville make animal sounds. First, I asked Gator, and he barked. Then I asked Gabby, and she meowed. The mystery was solved. They all wanted to be the teacher's pet!

Write one sentence that tells about a special person or place. Circle the proper noun. Sample answer given.

Mr. Greene is my principal.

Think of one more proper noun to add to your sentence. Rewrite the sentence. Sample answer given.

Mr. Greene is my principal at Critterville School.

Pronouns

Pronouns take the place of nouns. These replacements must be chosen very carefully. Some pronouns you might use are: I, me, you, he, she, him, it, we, us, they, them, my, mine, your, his, her, hers, its, ours, and their.

Examples:
Bat Child tells jokes. → He tells jokes.
Maurice and Molly are twins. → They are twins.
The car broke down. → It broke down.
Little Sister danced in a recital. → She danced in a recital.
______ worked hard. → I worked hard.
your name

Read Bat Child's riddles below. Circle every pronoun.

What should I say if I meet a monster with three heads?
"Hello. How are you? Hello. How are you? Hello. How are you?"

Why did the bat want to become a photographer?
She loved being in dark rooms.

Why did it take a bookworm ten months to finish a book?
He wasn't very hungry.

Read the paragraph below. Write a pronoun in each blank.

Maurice and Molly went to the store with their mother. They were getting a birthday gift for Little Critter. "I wonder what he would like?" asked their mother. "I think he would like a football," said Molly. "I think he would like some new paints and paper," said Maurice. Their mom said "Here is a Super Critter doll. It has a red cape and it talks when you pull this string. What do you think?" she asked. "That's cool! Let's get it!" said Maurice and Molly.

Write a sentence about a funny toy or a funny birthday present.

Sentences will vary.

Replace the noun you used above with a pronoun and rewrite your sentence.

Sentences will vary.

Verbs

Verbs are parts of speech that can show action. They tell what is happening. Without action verbs, nothing would get done!

Little Sister walked to the edge of the pool. She dipped her toe in to see if the water was cold. She held her nose and got ready to jump.

"Go on and jump," Dad told Little Sister. "I'll catch you!"

Read Little Sister's poem about the Critter's family vacation. Circle eight action verbs.

We went on vacation.
We saw lots of things.
We slept in a motel.
I played on the swings.

I pulled on my swimsuit.
I walked to the pool.
I jumped in the water.
I think I'm so cool.

Read the paragraph below about Little Critter's trip to an amusement park. Write an action verb in each blank.

Sample answer given.

My family and I visited Critterland. We spun around and around on our first ride. We rolled over and over on the next ride. When we got on the roller coaster, we zoomed up and down.

Write a sentence that tells what might happen at the amusement park next. Underline your action verb. Sample answer given.

We drove little cars around the curvy track.

Reread your sentence. Substitute a new action verb for the original verb. Rewrite the sentence. Underline the new action verb.

We steered little cars around the curvy track.

Action and Linking Verbs

Action verbs show action.

Little Critter washes the dishes.

Linking verbs help tell about the subject.

Little Critter is thoughtful.

Here are some examples of linking verbs:

am was is were are be

In the sentences below, circle the action verbs and draw a box around the linking verbs.

Little Critter peeled the carrots.
Little Sister washed the potatoes.
They were very helpful.
Mom cooked the vegetables.
Dad sliced the meat.
Everyone was hungry.
Blue waited under the table for scraps.
Little Critter handed Blue something to eat.
Dinner was delicious.
Blue thought so, too.

Make a list of **action verbs**. Try to think of at least three different words. Sample answers given.	Make a list of **linking verbs**. Sample answers given.
swim	am
ride	are
jump	was

Pick three of your action verbs. Use them in sentences below.

1. Sentences will vary.
2.
3.

Pick three of your linking verbs. Use them in sentences below.

1. Sentences will vary.
2.
3.

Review: Nouns, Pronouns, Verbs

Read the paragraph. Write a common noun in each blank.
Sample answers given.

Mom said that it was time to clean my room. I had not done this for two weeks, so it was a little messy. First, I looked under my bed. I was surprised to find my shoe! When I looked in the drawer, I saw my spider! When I opened the closet, my glove fell out!

Read the story below. Circle the seven proper nouns.

Maurice and Molly did not know what to do. Their favorite movie theater, Super Cinema was closed. They went to the Play Until Dark Park but it was closed. Finally, Maurice and Molly rode their bikes to the Critterville Library. The bike rack was full. Everyone else was looking for something to do, too.

QUIET PLEASE!!

Read the story below. Draw a line under each pronoun. Look back on page 116 if you need help remembering pronouns.

The knight was upset. He did not know what to do. The king and queen had asked him to find a dragon. They wanted to put it in the Royal Zoo. The poor knight sat down on a rock. He knew that no dragons existed. They had not lived for many years.

The knight sat for hours. No ideas came to him. Then a dragonfly landed next to him. He picked it up and brought it to the king and queen. They were happy. They had their dragon at last!

Read the sentences. Draw a circle around each verb.

1. Mom, Little Sister, and Little Critter made cookies.
2. Little Sister rolled out the dough.
3. Little Critter cut out the shapes with cookie cutters.
4. Then mom put them in the oven.
5. The cookies cooled on the counter.
6. Finally, everyone decorated the cookies and ate them.
7. They were delicious.

Adjectives

Adjectives describe nouns and pronouns. They are parts of speech that help paint a picture in your mind.

Little Critter's striped pajamas are black and white. Little Sister's spotted pajamas are orange and brown. Little Critter and Little Sister look like they belong at the zoo.

Read the story below. Circle the adjectives.

Miss Kitty is a good teacher. She took her class on a fascinating field trip to the zoo. It was a beautiful day. The sun was high in the bright blue sky. The students saw huge elephants, graceful giraffes, and peaceful zebras. They ate a delicious picnic lunch under an old oak tree and sang silly songs on the long bus ride home. Everybody had a great time and learned a lot.

After the field trip, Miss Kitty had her students write about their day. Help the children add some adjectives to their writing to make it more interesting. Write an adjective in each space. Draw a picture to match each sentence.
Sample answers given.

The yellow bus took us to the zoo. It was a bumpy ride.	We saw a colorful bird sitting in a big tree.
A striped snake slithered through the tall grass.	Some quiet zebras were eating brown grass for their dinner.

It was a super day. Miss Kitty is a wonderful teacher.

SPECTRUM

SPECTRUM WORKBOOKS ILLUSTRATED BY MERCER MAYER!

Grades K–2 • 128–160 full-color pages • Size: 8.375" x 10.875" • Paperback

McGraw-Hill, the premier educational publisher for grades PreK–12, and acclaimed children's author and illustrator, Mercer Mayer, are the proud creators of this workbook line featuring the lovable Little Critter. Like other Spectrum titles, the length, breadth, and depth of the activities in these workbooks enable children to learn a variety of skills about a single subject.

- Mercer Mayer's Little Critter family of characters has sold over 50 million books. These wholesome characters and stories appeal to both parents and teachers.
- Each full-color workbook is based on highly respected McGraw-Hill Companies' textbooks.
- All exercises feature easy-to-follow instructions.
- An answer key is included in each workbook.

TITLE	ISBN	PRICE
LANGUAGE ARTS		
Gr. K	1-57768-840-6	$8.95
Gr. 1	1-57768-841-4	$8.95
Gr. 2	1-57768-842-2	$8.95
MATH		
Gr. K	1-57768-800-7	$8.95
Gr. 1	1-57768-801-5	$8.95
Gr. 2	1-57768-802-3	$8.95
PHONICS		
Gr. K	1-57768-820-1	$8.95
Gr. 1	1-57768-821-X	$8.95
Gr. 2	1-57768-822-8	$8.95
READING		
Gr. K	1-57768-810-4	$8.95
Gr. 1	1-57768-811-2	$8.95
Gr. 2	1-57768-812-0	$8.95
SPELLING		
Gr. K	1-57768-830-9	$8.95
Gr. 1	1-57768-831-7	$8.95
Gr. 2	1-57768-832-5	$8.95
WRITING		
Gr. K	1-57768-850-3	$8.95
Gr. 1	1-57768-851-1	$8.95
Gr. 2	1-57768-852-X	$8.95

Prices subject to change without notice.

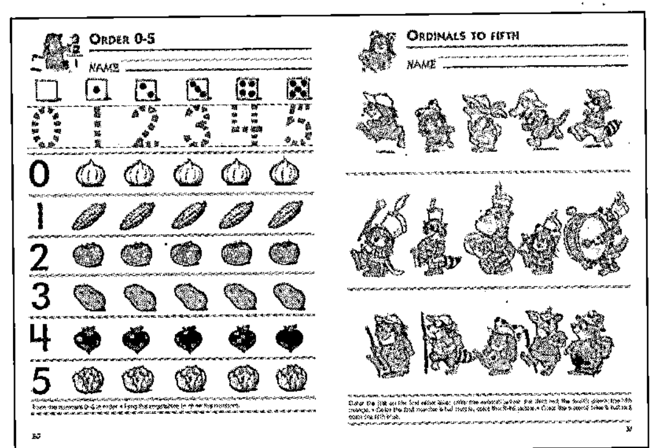

Wholesome, well-known characters plus proven school curriculum equals learning success!

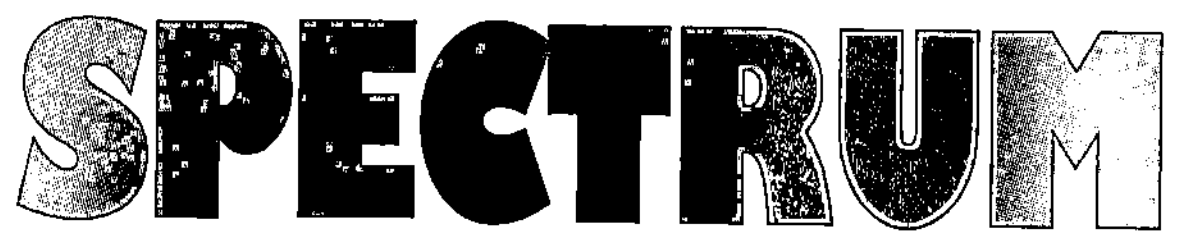

Brought to you by McGraw-Hill, the premier educational publisher for grades PreK–12. All our workbooks meet school curriculum guidelines and correspond to The McGraw-Hill Companies' classroom textbooks.

LANGUAGE ARTS

Grades 3–6 • 160 full-color pages
Size: 8.375" x 10.875" • Paperback

Encourages creativity and builds confidence by making writing fun! Sixty four-part lessons strengthen writing skills by focusing on parts of speech, word usage, sentence structure, punctuation, and proofreading. This series is based on the highly respected SRA/McGraw-Hill language arts series. Answer key included.

MATH

Grades K–8 • Over 150 pages
Size: 8.375" x 10.875" • Paperback

Features easy-to-follow instructions that give students a clear path to success. This series includes comprehensive coverage of the basic skills, helping children master math fundamentals. Answer key included.

PHONICS/WORD STUDY

Grades K–6 • Over 200 pages
Size: 8.375" x 10.875" • Paperback

Provides everything children need to build multiple skills in language arts. This series focuses on phonics, structural analysis, and dictionary skills, and offers creative ideas for using phonics and word study skills in language areas. Answer key included.

TITLE	ISBN	PRICE
LANGUAGE ARTS		
Gr. 3	1-57768-483-4	$8.95
Gr. 4	1-57768-484-2	$8.95
Gr. 5	1-57768-485-0	$8.95
Gr. 6	1-57768-486-9	$8.95
MATH		
Gr. K	1-57768-400-1	$8.95
Gr. 1	1-57768-401-X	$8.95
Gr. 2	1-57768-402-8	$8.95
Gr. 3	1-57768-403-6	$8.95
Gr. 4	1-57768-404-4	$8.95
Gr. 5	1-57768-405-2	$8.95
Gr. 6	1-57768-406-0	$8.95
Gr. 7	1-57768-407-9	$8.95
Gr. 8	1-57768-408-7	$8.95
PHONICS (Grades K–3)/WORD STUDY and PHONICS (Grades 4–6)		
Gr. K	1-57768-450-8	$8.95
Gr. 1	1-57768-451-6	$8.95
Gr. 2	1-57768-452-4	$8.95
Gr. 3	1-57768-453-2	$8.95
Gr. 4	1-57768-454-0	$8.95
Gr. 5	1-57768-455-9	$8.95
Gr. 6	1-57768-456-7	$8.95

Prices subject to change without notice.

SPECTRUM offers comprehensive coverage of basic skills.

READING

Grades K–6 • Over 150 full-color pages
Size: 8.375" x 10.875" • Paperback

This full-color series creates an enjoyable reading environment, even for below-average readers. Each book contains captivating content, colorful characters, and compelling illustrations, so children are eager to find out what happens next. Answer key included.

SPELLING

Grades 3–6 • 160 full-color pages
Size: 8.375" x 10.875" • Paperback

This full-color series links spelling to reading and writing, and increases skills in words and meanings, consonant and vowel spellings, and proofreading practice. Speller dictionary and answer key included.

TEST PREP

Grades 1–8 • 160 full-color pages
Size: 8.375" x 10.875" • Paperback

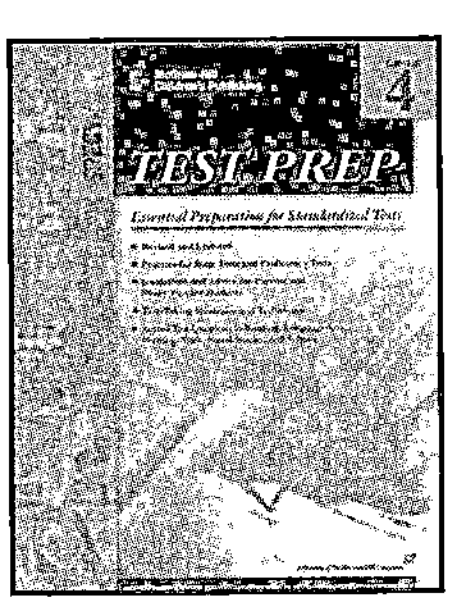

This series teaches the skills, strategies, and techniques necessary for students to succeed on any standardized test. Each book contains guidelines and advice for parents along with study tips for students. Grades 1 and 2 cover Reading, Language Arts, Writing, and Math. Grades 3 through 8 cover Reading, Language Arts, Writing, Math, Social Studies, and Science.

WRITING

Grades 3–6 • 160 full-color pages
Size: 8.375" x 10.875" • Paperback

Lessons focus on creative and expository writing using clearly stated objectives and pre-writing exercises. Eight essential reading skills are applied. Activities include main idea, sequence, comparison, detail, fact and opinion, cause and effect, making a point, and point of view. Each level includes a Writer's Handbook that offers writing tips. Answer key included.

FLASH CARDS

Card size: 3.0625" x 4.5625"

Flash cards provide children with one of the most effective ways to drill and practice fundamentals. The cards have large type, making it easy for young learners to read them. Each pack contains 50 flash cards including a parent instruction card that offers suggestions for fun, creative activities and games that reinforce children's skills development.

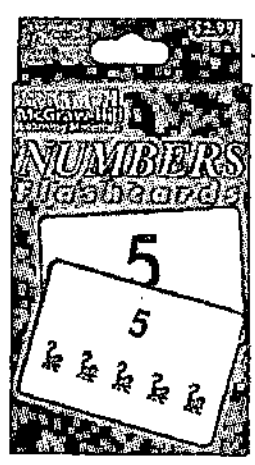

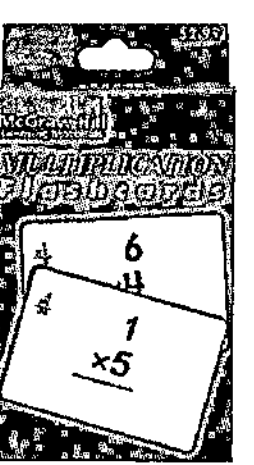

TITLE	ISBN	PRICE
READING		
Gr. K	1-57768-460-5	$8.95
Gr. 1	1-57768-461-3	$8.95
Gr. 2	1-57768-462-1	$8.95
Gr. 3	1-57768-463-X	$8.95
Gr. 4	1-57768-464-8	$8.95
Gr. 5	1-57768-465-6	$8.95
Gr. 6	1-57768-466-4	$8.95
SPELLING		
Gr. 3	1-57768-493-1	$8.95
Gr. 4	1-57768-494-X	$8.95
Gr. 5	1-57768-495-8	$8.95
Gr. 6	1-57768-496-6	$8.95
TEST PREP		
Gr. 1–2	1-57768-662-4	$9.95
Gr. 3	1-57768-663-2	$9.95
Gr. 4	1-57768-664-0	$9.95
Gr. 5	1-57768-665-9	$9.95
Gr. 6	1-57768-666-7	$9.95
Gr. 7	1-57768-667-5	$9.95
Gr. 8	1-57768-668-3	$9.95
WRITING		
Gr. 3	1-57768-913-5	$8.95
Gr. 4	1-57768-914-3	$8.95
Gr. 5	1-57768-915-1	$8.95
Gr. 6	1-57768-916-X	$8.95
FLASH CARDS		
Addition	1-57768-167-3	$2.99
Alphabet	1-57768-151-7	$2.99
Division	1-57768-158-4	$2.99
Money	1-57768-150-9	$2.99
Multiplication	1-57768-157-6	$2.99
Numbers	1-57768-127-4	$2.99
Phonics	1-57768-152-5	$2.99
Sight Words	1-57768-160-6	$2.99
Subtraction	1-57768-168-1	$2.99
Telling Time	1-57768-138-X	$2.99

Prices subject to change without notice.

FIRST READERS

MERCER MAYER FIRST READERS SKILLS AND PRACTICE

Levels 1, 2, 3 (Grades PreK–2) • 24 Pages • Size: 6" x 9" • Paperback

Young readers will enjoy these simple and engaging stories written with their reading level in mind. Featuring Mercer Mayer's charming illustrations and favorite Little Critter characters, these are the books children will want to read again and again. To ensure reading success, the First Readers are based on McGraw-Hill's respected educational SRA Open Court Reading Program. Skill-based activities in the back of the book also help reinforce learning. A word list is included for vocabulary practice. Each book contains 24 full-color pages.

Level 1 (Grades PreK–K)

TITLE	ISBN	PRICE
Camping Out	1-57768-806-6	$3.95
No One Can Play	1-57768-804-X	$3.95
Play Ball	1-57768-803-1	$3.95
Snow Day	1-57768-805-8	$3.95
Little Critter Slipcase 1 (Contains 4 titles; 1 each of the above titles)	1-57768-823-6	$15.95
Show and Tell	1-57768-835-X	$3.95
New Kid in Town	1-57768-829-5	$3.95
Country Fair	1-57768-827-9	$3.95
My Trip to the Zoo	1-57768-826-0	$3.95
Little Critter Slipcase 2 (Contains 4 titles; 1 each of the above titles)	1-57768-853-8	$15.95

Level 2 (Grades K–1)

TITLE	ISBN	PRICE
The Mixed-Up Morning	1-57768-808-2	$3.95
A Yummy Lunch	1-57768-809-0	$3.95
Our Park	1-57768-807-4	$3.95
Field Day	1-57768-813-9	$3.95
Little Critter Slipcase 1 (Contains 4 titles; 1 each of the above titles)	1-57768-824-4	$15.95
Beach Day	1-57768-844-9	$3.95
The New Fire Truck	1-57768-843-0	$3.95
A Day at Camp	1-57768-836-8	$3.95
Tiger's Birthday	1-57768-828-7	$3.95
Little Critter Slipcase 2 (Contains 4 titles; 1 each of the above titles)	1-57768-854-6	$15.95

Level 3 (Grades 1–2)

TITLE	ISBN	PRICE
Surprise!	1-57768-814-7	$3.95
Our Friend Sam	1-57768-815-5	$3.95
Helping Mom	1-57768-816-3	$3.95
My Trip to the Farm	1-57768-817-1	$3.95
Little Critter Slipcase 1 (Contains 4 titles; 1 each of the above titles)	1-57768-825-2	$15.95
Grandma's Garden	1-57768-846-5	$3.95
Class Trip	1-57768-845-7	$3.95
Goodnight, Little Critter	1-57768-834-1	$3.95
Our Tree House	1-57768-833-3	$3.95
Little Critter Slipcase 2 (Contains 4 titles; 1 each of the above titles)	1-57768-855-4	$15.95

Prices subject to change without notice.

The Children's Book Council has named **Snow Day** and **Our Friend Sam** recipients of the Council's "Children's Choices 2002" awards, placing the two titles among the highest recommended books for children.